The Comparative Method

Charles C. Ragin

THE COMPARATIVE METHOD
Moving Beyond Qualitative and Quantitative Strategies

UNIVERSITY
OF
CALIFORNIA
PRESS

BERKELEY
LOS ANGELES
LONDON

University of California Press
Berkeley and Los Angeles, California

University of California Press, Ltd.
London, England

© 1987 by
The Regents of the University of California

First Paperback Printing 1989

LIBRARY OF CONGRESS CATALOGING-IN-PUBLICATION DATA

Ragin, Charles C.
     The Comparative method.

     Bibliography: p.
     1. Social sciences — Comparative method. I. Title.
H61.R216 1987   300'.72   86-30800
ISBN 0-520-05834-8 (alk. paper)
ISBN 0-520-06618-9 (paperback)

Printed in the United States of America

2 3 4 5 6 7 8 9

1 2 3 4 5 6 7 8 9 (paperback)

Contents

Preface and Overview

My interest in developing and formalizing techniques of qualitative, holistic comparison originated in the frustrations I experienced as a comparative sociologist. I was trained, as are most American social scientists today, to use multivariate statistical techniques whenever possible. I often found, however, that these techniques were not well suited for answering some of the questions that interested me. For example, I often found that my theoretical and substantive interests led me to hypothesize relatively complex patterns of statistical interaction. Yet the cross-national data sets I was using were relatively small in size and severely constrained such analyses. A second problem concerned the comparability of different countries. When can two nation-states legitimately be compared? Statistical methods encourage investigators to increase sample size and ignore or at least skirt issues of comparability. I found this bias frustrating because it discourages investigators from asking questions about historically, culturally, or geographically defined social phenomena.

Instead of trying to develop new techniques appropriate for the questions that interested me, I first attempted to use traditional statistical methods whenever possible. Of course, I was not by myself. Today, social scientists routinely apply multivariate statistical techniques to any question with a large enough data base to allow their use. Often, the desire to use these techniques shapes the way social scientists ask their questions. Instead of asking questions about relatively narrow classes of phenomena (about types of national revolts, for instance), they tend to reformulate their questions so that they apply to wider categories (such as questions about cross-national variation in levels of political instability). Instead of trying to determine the different contexts in which a cause influences a certain outcome, they tend to assess a cause's average influence across a variety (preferably a diverse sample) of settings.

There is a long tradition in the social sciences of preferring big questions and comparably broad empirical generalizations. Thus, the reformulation of questions according to the demands of statistical techniques is generally applauded. This book represents an effort to step back from traditional statistical techniques, in comparative social science especially, and to explore alternatives. In doing this, I am bucking the trend in mainstream social science toward the application of ever more sophisticated multivariate techniques to all types of social data. Fortunately, I am not alone in this endeavor, and like others engaged in similar or parallel struggles (see Duncan 1984, Lieberson 1985, Stinchcombe 1978, and Tilly 1984), I remain sympathetic with (and an avid user of) multivariate statistical techniques. The problem is not to show which methodology is best but to explore alternative ways of establishing a meaningful dialogue between ideas and evidence.

Initially, my only goal in this work was to present a preliminary formulation of a technique of data reduction that uses Boolean algebra to simplify complex data structures in a logical and holistic manner. I found, however, that it was very difficult to present the technique I had developed without also presenting a general discussion of strategies of comparative research. Not only is this discussion crucial as background material; it repeats, in a highly simplified form, the intellectual journey that led to the development of an algebraic technique of qualitative comparison. By itself, the technique is only a set of relatively simple algorithms. When considered in the context of problems in comparative research and social science methodology more generally, however, the logic of the qualitative comparative approach becomes clear.

Comparative social science is an ideal setting for addressing basic methodological issues. The essential characteristics of the qualitative/quantitative split in the social sciences are clearly visible in comparative social science. In contrast to other subdisciplines, this field has a long tradition of qualitative work that is stronger and richer than its quantitative counterpart. Not only is this tradition qualitative, but it also tends to be case-oriented (as opposed to variable-oriented) and historical (as opposed to abstractly causal). For these reasons the split between the two major research strategies is more complete and more profound in comparative social science than in most other subdisciplines.

The consequences of this division are unmistakable and unfortunate. Important research questions are often overlooked, or if asked they tend to be distorted. For example, there are several cross-national studies of aggregate social turmoil involving virtually all countries, and there are comparative case studies of the handful of countries that have experienced social revolutions, but the cross-national studies tend to be vague and abstract, and the studies of social revolution tend to treat each revolution separately and draw only a few general conclusions. The tendency is either to expand research questions so that they are broader and therefore relevant to many countries or to restrict investigation to a few significant cases. Interest in military coups in Africa, for example, might be expanded into a study of regime instability and encompass all Third World countries (or all countries), or it might be confined to an in-depth analysis of a manageably small number of major military coups.

The first approach, broadening the scope of a study, is attractive because it allows the use of the quantitative tools of mainstream social science. The problem with this practice, which I characterize as a variable-oriented approach, is that in the course of satisfying the demands of statistical techniques, the connection between the research, on the one hand, and the theoretical, substantive, and political concerns that motivate research in the first place, on the other, tends to be strained. Sometimes quantitative cross-national studies have an unreal quality to them—countries become organisms with systemic distress, for example—and the data examined have little meaningful connection to actual empirical processes. More concrete questions—relevant to the social bases and origins of specific phenomena in similarly situated countries and regions—do not receive the attention they deserve.

These questions usually are addressed only by researchers who study a few cases at a time. I refer to this second approach, which tends to be qualitative, as the case-oriented tradition. Case-oriented studies, by their nature, are sensitive to complexity and historical specificity. Thus, they are well suited for addressing empirically defined historical outcomes, and they are often used to generate new conceptual schemes, as well. Researchers who are oriented toward specific cases (area specialists especially) do not find it difficult to maintain a meaningful connection to social and political issues because they are more concerned with actual events, with human agency and process. It is difficult, however, to sustain attention to complexity across a large number of cases. Furthermore, case-oriented researchers are always open to the charge that their findings are specific to the few cases they examine, and when they do make broad comparisons and attempt to generalize, they often are accused of letting their favorite cases shape or at least color their generalizations.

While the case-oriented approach is limited in this way, it has many special features that are well worth preserving, even in studies that span many cases. First, case-oriented methods are holistic—they treat cases as whole entities and not as collections of parts (or as collections of scores on variables). Thus, the relations between the parts of a whole are understood within the context of the whole, not within the context of general patterns of covariation between variables characterizing the members of a population of comparable units. Second, causation is understood conjuncturally. Outcomes are analyzed in terms of intersections of conditions, and it is usually assumed that any of several combinations of conditions might produce a certain outcome. These and other features of case-oriented methods make it possible for investigators to interpret cases historically and make statements about the origins of important qualitative changes in specific settings.

A primary goal of this book is to identify the unique strengths of case-oriented methods and to formalize them as a general method of qualitative comparison using Boolean algebra. The analytic strategy I present (which I call the qualitative comparative method) can be applied to a few cases or to hundreds. The principle guiding the formulation of this approach was that the essential features of case-oriented methods should be preserved as much as possible in the development of techniques for larger questions. This is important because mainstream statistical methods disaggregate cases into variables and distributions before analyzing them. This practice makes historical interpretive work very difficult, if not impossible. In short, my goal was to formalize qualitative comparative methods without departing from the general logic of case-oriented research. The formalization I present is based on Boolean algebra, the algebra of logic and set theory.

In many respects, the analytic strategy I discuss provides an alternative to multivariate statistical analysis. Unlike multivariate statistical analysis, which tends to be radically analytic (because it breaks cases into parts—variables—that are difficult to reassemble into wholes), qualitative comparison allows examination of constellations, configurations, and conjunctures. It is especially well suited for addressing questions about outcomes resulting from multiple and conjunctural causes—where different conditions combine in different and sometimes contradictory ways to produce the same or similar outcomes. Multivariate statistical techniques start with simplifying assumptions about causes and their interrelation as variables. The method of qualitative comparison, by contrast, starts by assuming maximum causal complexity and then mounts an assault on that complexity.

While the techniques I present could be considered alternatives to multivariate statistical analysis, they do not supersede traditional statistical methods. In fact, experience may show that they can be used to greatest advantage in conjunction with them. An important part of research is the dialogue that develops between the investigator's theory and the data. Generally, the character of this dialogue is shaped by the techniques of data analysis used by the investigator. While this dialogue occurs in all types of social scientific research, in comparative social science, especially in the branch I call case-oriented, it is particularly rich and elaborate. The techniques of qualitative comparison that I introduce bring some of this richness to studies involving more than a handful of cases. In other words, they overcome some of the limitations of multivariate statistical techniques as a basis for carrying on this dialogue. Thus, use of these techniques may be viewed as a possible corrective to the radically analytic tendencies of most statistical techniques.

This work addresses specific methodological issues in comparative social science, issues I have worked on over the last several years. However, the methodological problems I address and the tentative solutions I offer are not in any way restricted to the fields of comparative sociology and political science, where I draw most of my examples. I discuss two research traditions in comparative social science. One traditionally has been viewed as qualitative, the other as quantitative. This division occurs again and again in virtually every social scientific field; it is certainly not restricted to comparative work. Essentially, I address metatheoretical differences between approaches generally called qualitative (or case-oriented) and quantitative (or variable-oriented)—primarily in terms of their different orientations toward the analysis and interpretation of data. Less attention is paid in this work to the production of so-called raw data, an integral part of the research process.

AN IMPORTANT CAVEAT

The Boolean approach developed in this work touches the world of statistical analysis of social data in several ways. It examines cases; it uses categorical variables; it looks at different combinations of conditions (that is, cells of a multivariate cross-tabulation); it can be applied to categorical dependent variables; and it involves data reduction. Thus, it should not be surprising that I have encountered strong pressure to build a bridge between the Boolean approach and statistical methods designed for these kinds of data and problems (such as log-linear methods) in order to show how the two approaches can be usefully integrated.

This bridge can be made under certain conditions (for example, availability of a very large number of observations), but this book is not the place for it. If I were to present that bridge in this work, many readers would conclude that the case-oriented approach is simply a watered-down version of log-linear statistical methodology. It is essential, however, to acknowledge and comprehend the unique features of the case-oriented approach. One of my primary goals is to broaden the boundaries of methodological discussion by formalizing the differences between case-oriented and variable-oriented research in comparative social science and other subdisciplines as well.

Some sections of the work may be read defensively by those who use statistical methods regularly, and technical solutions to some of the problems I discuss will immediately come to mind. My primary point in these discussions is not to argue that these problems cannot be solved by statistical methods but to show that by their nature statistical methods tend to discourage awareness of these problems. I am not concerned that the use of statistical techniques requires assumptions, for example, but I am troubled by the tendency for these assumptions to become hidden from the user's view and to distort the dialogue between ideas and evidence.

WHAT FOLLOWS

Chapter 1 discusses the distinctive features of comparative social science, especially its case-oriented tradition, that make it an ideal setting for examining basic methodological issues. Prominent among these features are its qualitative orientation and its related interest in (and appreciation of) complexity, its emphasis on interpretive questions and specific historical outcomes and processes, its limited data base (many questions are relevant to only a small number of countries or regions), and its special metatheoretical treatment of aggregate units such as nation-states. For these and related reasons, the consequences of methodological decisions are more apparent in comparative research than in other areas.

A hallmark of qualitative approaches is their attention to complexity—the heterogeneity and particularity of individual cases. Chapter 2 addresses the problem of complexity through a discussion of multiple conjunctural causation and the special methodological problems this type of causation presents. When several different combinations of conditions produce the same outcome (a common finding in comparative studies), it is very difficult to unravel the different patterns across a range of cases. Analysis is further complicated by the limited diversity of naturally occurring social phenomena. (In a laboratory it is possible to manufacture all possible combinations of causes and thereby disentangle the decisive causal conjunctures.) Chapter 2 outlines this basic problem in order to set the stage for discussing the two dominant ways of simplifying complexity—by examining similarities and differences among a limited number of cases (the case-oriented strategy) and by looking at relations between variables (the variable-oriented strategy).

The first major strategy, the case-oriented approach, is the focus of Chapter 3. A common goal in this type of analysis is to interpret a common historical outcome or process across a limited range of cases, usually only a handful. Cases are examined as wholes, which means that the causal significance of an event or structure depends on the context (that is, on other features of the case). This strategy highlights complexity, diversity, and uniqueness, and it provides a powerful basis for interpreting cases historically. However, it is very difficult to use this approach to examine more than a few cases at a time. Faced with a large number of cases, the investigator is forced to make many paired comparisons—too many to grasp all at once—and the analysis may disintegrate into descriptive statements lacking any generality. Thus, while the case-oriented approach avoids many of the simplifying assumptions of the variable-oriented approach, it cannot be used to address similarities and differences among many cases.

The variable-oriented approach, the focus of Chapter 4, is the dominant research strategy of mainstream social science. In this approach cases are disaggregated into variables and distributions. Examination of patterns of covariation among variables is used as a basis for making general statements about relations between aspects of cases considered collectively as populations of comparable observations. These general statements typically are linked to abstract theoretical ideas about generic properties of macrosocial units (such as societies). Because this strategy starts with simplifying assumptions, it is a powerful data reducer. Thus, it is an ideal instrument for producing broad statements pertaining to relatively large bodies of data encompassing diverse cases. However, the simplifying assumptions that make this approach possible often violate commonsense notions of causation and sometimes pose serious obstacles to making interpretive statements about specific cases or even about categories of cases.

A conceivable resolution of the gulf between case-oriented and variable-oriented research is to combine the two strategies in some way. In fact, many investigators have attempted to do this with moderate success. Chapter 5 analyzes three such attempts: Jeffrey Paige's *Agrarian Revolution*, John Stephens's *The Transition from Capitalism to Socialism*, and Edward Shorter and Charles Tilly's *Strikes in France*. These three studies have many laudable features, but their respective research strategies do not fully transcend the quantitative/qualitative split in comparative social science. Even though all three combine variable-oriented and case-oriented methods, each tends to be dominated by one strategy. Paige's study and Stephens's study are primarily variable-oriented approaches buttressed with independent case studies, while Shorter and Tilly's work is primarily a case study that uses quantitative analysis to support their broad historical interpretation of that case.

The discussion of combined strategies provides a basis for outlining the essential features of a more synthetic approach to comparative research. Basically, a synthetic strategy must be able to address more than a handful of cases and, at the same time, avoid making the simplifying assumptions about cause which are characteristic of the variable-oriented approach. It is essential to avoid certain simplifying assumptions because they interfere with the goal of historical interpretation. It is difficult to make statements about the origins of important historical outcomes, for example, if the model of causation implicit in the analytic technique contradicts theoretical and substantive understanding of the phenomenon in question. A synthetic, broadly comparative strategy must be both holistic—so that the cases themselves are not lost in the research process—and analytic—so that more than a few cases can be comprehended and modest generalization is possible.

An algebraic basis for a synthetic approach exists in Boolean algebra, the algebra of sets and logic. Chapter 6 presents the basic features of Boolean algebra (the Boolean number system, Boolean addition and multiplication, and set theory) and then introduces rudimentary principles of Boolean algebra used to logically minimize (reduce the complexity of) truth tables. The process of minimizing truth tables has a direct link to the problem of data reduction in variable-oriented research (a truth table bears some similarity to a data matrix), but the mechanics are entirely different. Chapter 6 details these differences. No background in Boolean algebra is assumed, and the notational system is simple.

The material presented in Chapter 7 builds on the previous chapter to introduce advanced methods of Boolean analysis. Two in particular are emphasized. The first addresses the limited diversity of social phenomena (that is, the fact that macrosocial phenomena cannot be manipulated experimentally). With Boolean techniques it is possible to construct a model of the diversity that exists among comparable outcomes and then to study the causes of these outcomes within the context of the "available" diversity. In other words, an integral part of the research process itself can involve direct attention to, and consideration of, the limitations of naturally occurring social phenomena. A second procedure concerns the use of set theory to contrast empirical configurations with theoretically constructed models. Essentially, this method makes it possible both to evaluate theories and to use them as a basis for historical interpretation. The major objective here is to show that Boolean methods are not mechanical techniques but can be integrated into the dialogue of ideas and evidence in social research.

Chapter 8 presents a variety of examples of Boolean-based qualitative analysis. The major example is an analysis of ethnic political mobilization among territorially based linguistic minorities in Western Europe. Others include an analysis of characteristics of juvenile courts and a reanalysis of data used by Stein Rokkan in presenting his configurational approach in comparative political sociology. Chapter 8 offers a range of examples to demonstrate the general utility of Boolean techniques of qualitative comparison. The examples are only preliminary because the larger argument emphasizes the role of qualitative comparative methods in the dialogue of ideas and evidence in social research, especially in comparative work that is both historically interpretive and causal-analytic. While it is impossible to reproduce an entire research dialogue in a brief illustration of method, I hope to convey the general flavor of this dialogue in the variety of examples presented.

Chapter 9 concludes the book by summarizing the major arguments and then emphasizing the strengths of Boolean techniques of qualitative comparison. It also discusses the impact of the application of Boolean techniques on the entire research process.

Acknowledgments

The current climate in the social sciences remains open to broad methodological discussion. The Department of Sociology at Northwestern University is an especially conducive setting for asking difficult and troubling questions. I am indebted to the entire department for its unique ambience. I am especially grateful for the detailed comments provided by my colleagues Arthur Stinchcombe and John Stephens on early drafts of this manuscript and to many other colleagues at Northwestern—especially Janet Abu-Lughod, Howard Becker, Arnold Feldman, Jack Goldstone, Christopher Jencks, Charles Moskos, and Christopher Winship—for their many helpful suggestions and moral support. Also, York Bradshaw and Jeremy Hein offered a lot of suggestions and assisted with some of the more mundane aspects of producing this document.

I would also like to thank a number of former colleagues at Indiana University, especially Larry Griffin, David Zaret, Bill Corsaro, and Tom Gieryn. Scholars elsewhere also have provided useful comments and advice. Among them are Daniel Chirot, Kriss Drass, and John Walton. John Walton, in particular, offered many detailed suggestions and much needed encouragement in the final stages of writing. I am very indebted to him for his help. The readers for the University of California Press provided excellent advice. Last but not least, I am also thankful to the American Bar Foundation and the Center for Urban Affairs and Policy Research for their financial support of my investigation of broad issues in social science methodology.

This book is dedicated to my wife, Ann, who has shared with me the challenge of turning my disordered thoughts into an intellectual statement. The completion of this work is testimony to her patience, her understanding, and her insight.

1

The Distinctiveness of
Comparative Social Science

"Thinking without comparison is unthinkable. And, in the absence of comparison, so is all scientific thought and scientific research" (Swanson 1971 : 145). Most social scientists today would agree with this observation, although some might be tempted to substitute the phrase *variables and relationships* for the word *comparison*. Virtually all empirical social research involves comparison of some sort. Researchers compare cases to each other; they use statistical methods to construct (and adjust) quantitative comparisons; they compare cases to theoretically derived pure cases; and they compare cases' values on relevant variables to average values in order to assess covariation. Comparison provides a basis for making statements about empirical regularities and for evaluating and interpreting cases relative to substantive and theoretical criteria. In this broad sense, comparison is central to empirical social science as it is practiced today. Lieberson (1985 : 44) states simply that social research, "in one form or other, is *comparative* research."

While virtually all social scientific methods are comparative in this broad sense, in social science the term *comparative method* typically is used in a narrow sense to refer to a specific kind of comparison—the comparison of large macrosocial units. In fact, the comparative method traditionally has been treated as the core method of comparative social science, the branch of social science concerned with cross-societal differences and similarities (Easthope 1974). Despite this tradition, there is substantial disagreement today concerning the distinctiveness of comparative social science in general

1

and the comparative method in particular. Several comparativists have objected to the idea that comparative social science is distinctive in any important respects from social science in general (Grimshaw 1973 : 18).

Smelser (1976 : 2–3), for example, claims that comparative social scientific inquiry is not a "species of inquiry independent from the remainder of social scientific inquiry" and that "the analysis of phenomena in evidently dissimilar units (especially different societies or cultures) should have no methodological problem unique to itself." According to Smelser (1976 : 5), this continuity between comparative and noncomparative work exists because their respective goals are identical—to explain social phenomena by establishing controls over the conditions and causes of variation. (See also Armer 1973 : 50.) Any technique that furthers the goal of explaining variation, according to this reasoning, is a comparative method. This includes virtually all analytic methods used by social scientists (see Bailey 1982).

This position, that there is nothing truly distinctive about comparative social science and that virtually all social scientific methods are comparative methods, is sound, and it is attractive because it suggests that social science subdisciplines are united by their methods. The argument is favored by many comparativists, in fact, because the emphasis on continuities between comparative and noncomparative work supports the idea that comparative social science is as scientific as its siblings. This position overlooks the fact, however, that there are important differences between the *orientations* of most comparativists and most noncomparativists and these differences have important methodological consequences. While it is true that the logic of social science is continuous from one subdiscipline to another, the peculiarities of comparative social science make it an ideal setting for an examination of key issues in methodology. In fact, I argue that a lot can be gained from exaggerating the distinctive aspects of comparative work and that these lessons can be applied to other social science subdisciplines as well.

The most distinctive aspect of comparative social science is the wide gulf between qualitative and quantitative work. It is wider in comparative social science than in perhaps any other social science subdiscipline. In part this is because its qualitative tradition is dominant, the opposite of the situation in most other fields. Over the last twenty years, some of the most celebrated works in the social sciences (from Moore's *Social Origins of Dictatorship and Democracy* to Wallerstein's *Modern World System*) have come out of this tradition, making it appear continuous with the grand theorizing of such classical scholars as Durkheim and Weber.

More fundamental to the gulf, however, is the fact that several other divisions coincide with the qualitative/quantitative split in comparative social science and reinforce it. Qualitative researchers tend to look at cases as wholes, and they compare whole cases with each other. While cases may be analyzed in terms of variables (for example, the presence or absence of a certain institution might be an important variable), cases are viewed as configurations—as combinations of characteristics. Comparison in the qualitative tradition thus involves comparing configurations. This holism contradicts the radically analytic approach of most quantitative work.

Not only is the qualitative tradition oriented toward cases as wholes, as configurations, but it also tends to be historically interpretive. The term *interpretive* is used in a restricted sense here. Often, the term is used to describe a type of social science that is only remotely empirical and concerned primarily with problems of meaning or hermeneutics. In this book, interpretive work is treated as a type of empirical social science: historically oriented interpretive work attempts to account for specific historical outcomes or sets of comparable outcomes or processes chosen for study because of their significance for current institutional arrangements or for social life in general. Typically, such work seeks to make sense out of different cases by piecing evidence together in a manner sensitive to chronology and by offering limited historical generalizations that are both objectively possible and cognizant of enabling conditions and limiting means—of context. This definition of interpretive work leans heavily on Weber (1949, 1975, 1977) but makes more allowance for the possibility of historical generalization based on examination of comparable cases. In this chapter I discuss these distinctive characteristics and sketch the implications of these features for comparative methodology. I begin by delineating the field.

THE BOUNDARIES AND GOALS OF COMPARATIVE SOCIAL SCIENCE

There have been several attempts to delineate the boundaries of comparative social science. Yet, there is still little agreement today concerning its domain. Most attempts to delineate the field have emphasized its special data or its special types of data. For reasons detailed below, this is a poor starting point. I argue that comparative social science is better defined by its distinctive goals.

It is common to define comparative research as research that uses comparable data from at least two societies. This definition emphasizes the fact that the data of comparative social science are cross-societal. (See Andreski 1965 : 66; Armer 1973 : 49.) While this is an acceptable working definition of comparative social science, most comparativists would find this definition too restrictive. It excludes, for example, comparatively oriented case studies. Tocqueville's *Democracy in America* is excluded, as is Durkheim's *Elementary Forms of the Religious Life*. Many area specialists are thoroughly comparative because they implicitly compare their chosen case to their own country or to an imaginary but theoretically decisive ideal-typic case. Thus, to define comparative social science in terms of its special data is a misleadingly concrete way to delineate its boundaries.

Others have attempted to differentiate comparative social science by emphasizing its multilevel character (as in Rokkan 1966 : 19–20). According to Przeworski and Teune (1970 : 50–51), comparative work proceeds at two levels simultaneously—at the level of systems (or macrosocial level) and at the within-system level. According to their argument, any analysis that is based only on macrosocial similarities and differences is not truly comparative, even if this analysis includes an examination of aggregations of within-system characteristics. For example, if an investigator uses system-level variables (such as GNP per capita) to explain variation in a dependent variable based on aggregations of individual-level data within each system (such as literacy rates), the study would not qualify as a comparative study according to Przeworski and Teune. Ideally, system-level variables should be used to explain variation across systems in within-system relationships.

Alford's (1963) study of international variation in class voting qualifies as a comparative study by these criteria because he uses system-level variables (degree of industrialization and urbanization) to explain differences among countries in within-system relationships (the strength of the relationship between social class and party support). Walton's (1984) study of national revolts in the Third World also conforms to this definition of comparative work. He uses degree of incorporation into the world economy, a system-level variable, to account for variation in the degree to which popular protests and state reactions to protest contributed to the coalescence of revolutionary situations in six countries (see especially Walton 1984 : 188–197). Few studies traditionally thought of as comparative, however, conform to these strictures. Comparatively oriented case studies are excluded, as are quantitative cross-national studies that use only aggregate, national-level data. (Note that quantitative cross-national studies focus directly on cross-societal similarities and differences.) Przeworski and Teune's definition of comparative inquiry as multilevel research is much more restrictive than even the first definition considered here.

Both definitions are inadequate. Yet they suggest a tentative solution to the problem of delineating comparative work. One level that invariably plays a big part in definitions of comparative work is the macrosocial level. It appears in the first definition offered above in its emphasis on data from two societies and in the second's emphasis on multilevel analyses, with one level the macrosocial. The boundaries of comparative social science, therefore, must be coterminous with a specific usage of macrosocial units.

It is not as a data category that macrosocial units are important to comparativists, but as a metatheoretical category. What distinguishes comparative social science is its use of attributes of macrosocial units in explanatory statements. This special usage is intimately linked to the twin goals of comparative social science—both to explain and to interpret macrosocial variation.

The importance of macrosocial units to explanation in comparative social science is best understood by example. Consider an investigation which concludes that a strong relationship between social class and party preference exists in Great Britain because "Great Britain is an industrial society." This conclusion concretizes the term *society* by providing an example (Great Britain) and by implying that there are other societies, some of which are industrial and some of which are not. If the investigator had concluded instead that the relationship exists because "citizens vote their pocketbooks" or because "the relations of production shape political consciousness," then he or she would have avoided concretizing any macrosocial unit and thereby would have avoided engaging in comparative social science.

This direct, empirical implementation of abstract, macrosocial units is a metatheoretical act, and it separates comparativists from noncomparativists. In order to compare societies or any other macrosocial unit, the comparativist must identify them by name. The comparativist thus assumes, at least implicitly, that macrosocial units are real and then defines them, sometimes by default, in the course of research. The fact that the difference between comparativists and noncomparativists is a metatheoretical difference based on the special goals of comparative social science has been obscured by the tendency of all social scientists to claim that they study societies or that social science is the study of society. For the noncomparativists, however, macrosocial units tend to remain abstractions. Noncomparativists can assure themselves that the patterns and processes they study exist in a society; the concept need not be operationalized explicitly. For the comparativists, however, macrosocial units impinge on their work in a fundamental manner.

Rarely are these large, encompassing units defined. (Parsons 1977 and Marsh 1967 are exceptions.) In his discussion of the distinctiveness of comparative work, for example, Grimshaw (1973 : 4) states, "I will defer discussion of what constitutes a [macrosocial] system." This reluctance is not uncommon; most comparativists are more interested in making comparisons than in defining the objects of their comparisons (see Andreski 1965 : 66). The fact remains, however, that comparativists compare macrosocial units; they must be operationalized in the course of comparative work.

At a very general level, comparativists are interested in identifying the similarities and differences among macrosocial units. This knowledge provides the key to understanding, explaining, and interpreting diverse historical outcomes and processes and their significance for current institutional arrangements. Cross-societal similarities and differences for many social scientists constitute the most significant feature of the social landscape, and, consequently, these researchers have an unmistakable preference for explanations that cite macrosocial phenomena. This tendency is reinforced by the fact that the goals of comparative social scientists typically extend beyond an interest in simply cataloging and explaining cross-societal similarities and differences. Most comparativists, especially those who are qualitatively oriented, also seek to interpret specific experiences and trajectories of specific countries (or categories of countries). That is, they are interested in the cases themselves, their different historical experiences in particular, not simply in relations between variables characterizing broad categories of cases. This interest reinforces the tendency to use macrosocial attributes in explanatory statements.

The decision to study macrosocial variation and to use explanatory statements citing macrosocial properties is, of course, a conscious choice, shaped in large part by the enduring reality of countries, nations, states, and other large (and imposing) political entities. As long as social scientists continue to be influenced by their social and historical contexts and continue to try to interpret them, they will use macrosocial attributes in their explanations of social phenomena. It is possible to imagine a social science devoid of explanatory statements citing macrosocial phenomena. A totally psychologized social science, for example, might attempt to disavow such explanations. It is unlikely, however, that social scientists will lose interest in interpreting national and international events and processes and thereby divorce themselves from significant features of their social contexts. (In any event, to do so would be to deny the social origins and bases of social science.) Thus, macrosocial units are central to the practice of comparative social science because they are an essential ingredient of the explanations comparativists offer.

A NOTE OF CAUTION ON UNITS OF ANALYSIS

It would be wrong at this point to conclude simply that comparativists differ from noncomparativists in their "chosen unit of analysis." The example supplied previously suggests that any data unit can be used in comparative research. All that matters is how the results of research are understood. The fact that the explanations of comparative social science tend to be cross-societal and cite macrosocial phenomena, however, implies that the question of units is relevant.

Very little continuity exists, however, in discussions of units of analysis offered by comparatively oriented social scientists. An important source of this lack of continuity is the simple fact that the term *unit of analysis* is used to describe two very distinct metatheoretical constructs. Sometimes unit of analysis is used in reference to data categories. In a quantitative cross-national study of economic dependency and economic development, for example, an investigator might state that the unit of analysis is the nation-state because the data are collected at that level. At other times, however, the term *unit of analysis* is used in reference to theoretical categories. Wiener (1976), for example, in a review of Barrington Moore's *Social Origins of Dictatorship and Democracy* (1966), states that Moore's unit of analysis is "class." Wallerstein (1974, 1979, 1980, 1984) argues in various works that there is only one valid unit of analysis in comparative social science: the "world system." Upon closer examination, however, one finds that Moore's cases are different countries and Wallerstein's discussion of the modern world system is rife with references to nation-states and comparisons of, for example, core countries and peripheral countries.

The fact that the term *unit of analysis* has been used in reference to both data categories and theoretical categories has created a great deal of confusion in the field of comparative social science. Some followers of Wallerstein, for example, have attacked those who use the nation-state as a unit of analysis in the data category sense, arguing that this practice violates world-systems theory and results in meaningless tests of its propositions. (See, for example, Bach 1977.) Other researchers have attempted to use the modern world system as a unit of analysis in the data category sense and have examined cycles and trends in the world economy as a whole. (See, for example, Bergesen 1980 and McGowan 1985.) It is clear from Wallerstein's discussion and from his actual analyses of the world system, however, that his argument is that the world system is the only valid explanatory unit, not the only valid data unit.

This tension between the two meanings of unit of analysis has bedevilled the comparative social science literature at least since the early 1960s. Issues associated with the aggregation problem have compounded the terminological difficulties and confusion. Allardt (1966 : 339–341), for example, attempted to draw a distinction between "data units" and "analytical units," arguing that the latter are more theoretically relevant. In a similar vein, Scheuch (1966 : 164) argued that comparativists should distinguish between "units of observation" (see also Walton 1973 : 176) and "units of inference." In an early attempt to formulate a methodological position, Hopkins and Wallerstein (1970 : 183) contrasted "research sites" and "theoretical units." Several researchers attempted to clarify the situation by limiting their comments to "units of comparison" (Eisenstadt 1966 : 86; Etzioni and Dubow 1970 : 7; Czudnowski 1976 : 27). Finally, Przeworski and Teune (1970 : 8, 49–50) attempted to distinguish between "levels of observation" and "levels of analysis."

Most of these discussions were stimulated by the ambiguity associated with the term *unit of analysis.* For most noncomparative social scientists, the term presents no special problems. Their analyses and their explanations typically proceed at one level, the individual or organizational level. This is rarely the case in comparative social science, where the analysis often proceeds at one level (perhaps the individual level, as in the preceding example) and the explanation is couched at another level (usually the macrosocial level). Of course, this duality exists in other types of social science, and the methodological issues raised here apply to these areas as well. The duality is most pronounced, however, in comparative social science, which is one of the features that makes it an ideal arena for methodological discussion.

To clarify the unit of analysis question in comparative social science, it is necessary to distinguish between observational units and explanatory units. This distinction follows my discussion concerning the two meanings of unit of analysis—as a data category and as a theoretical category. *Observational unit* refers to the unit used in data collection and data analysis; *explanatory unit* refers to the unit that is used to account for the pattern of results obtained. In the class voting example mentioned above, the observational unit is the individual (the relationship is based on individual-level data) and the explanatory unit is societal.

METHODOLOGICAL CONSEQUENCES

The explanation that there is a strong relationship between social class and party preference in a sample of British voters because "Great Britain is an industrial society" implies that societies can be identified, that they can be classified as either industrial or not industrial, and that in industrial societies there is a strong relationship between social class and party preference, while in nonindustrial societies there is no such relationship. Because societies are (at least apparently) identifiable, an investigator conceivably could draw up a list of them, classify them as industrial and not industrial (or at least measure the degree to which each society is industrial), and then examine the degree to which the more industrial societies agree in manifesting a consistent relationship between social class and party choice and also the degree to which the less industrial societies agree in manifesting a weaker relationship. If these two patterns of agreement can be established, then the general statement (that in industrial societies there is a strong relationship between social class and party preference) used to explain the particular instance (the relationship observed in Great Britain) is supported.

Unfortunately, social scientific investigation is rarely this simple. There are many practical problems associated with establishing cross-societal demonstrations such as the one described above. Most of these practical problems concern the comparability of relatively dissimilar societies. This concern for comparability derives ultimately from the fact that the cases (say, countries) which comparativists study have known histories and identities. They are not anonymous, disembodied observations. In the preceding investigation, for instance, a researcher familiar with the relevant cases might have doubts about the cross-societal comparability of measures of class positions or about the identification of parties with social classes. An investigator might also have doubts about the classification of societies as industrial and not industrial or about ordinal and interval measures of degree of industrialization. These measurement problems are very important, and they have absorbed the attention of comparative social scientists for some time. In fact, many discussions of comparative methods have concerned these issues almost exclusively.

At a more basic level, it is difficult to evaluate explanatory statements of comparative social science because the number of relevant units available for such assessments is often limited by empirical constraints. Even the investigator who claims that he or she is interested in all societies, and defines societies as all contemporary nation-states, encounters serious statistical problems if a quantitative analysis of these cases is attempted. A seemingly large set of more than one hundred nation-states can be reduced by half if there are problems with missing data. Often, the remaining cases are not representative of the original hundred-plus nation-states, much less of all societies (or all macrosocial systems). This problem is apparent in the hypothetical research described above. There are many societies, both industrial and nonindustrial, that are not democratic. Thus, any attempt to assess the strength of the relationship between social class and party preference in these countries would be questionable, if not misguided. Furthermore, the definition of democratic society is problematic and ideologically charged.

Theoretical strictures also may reduce the number of relevant cases. In the hypothetical analysis of more and less industrial societies discussed above, for example, it is possible that the general statement (that social class shapes party preference only in industrial societies) is theoretically meaningful only when applied to democratic countries with a feudal past. If this were the case, then the investigator would first draw up a list of democracies with a feudal past and then distinguish between more and less industrial countries within this set. Generally speaking, the greater the theoretical or empirical specificity, the smaller the number of cases relevant to the investigation. The smaller the number of relevant cases, the greater the likelihood that the investigator will find it difficult to evaluate an explanatory statement in a way that conforms to the standards of mainstream social science, especially its quantitative branch.

Sometimes there are more explanations of a certain phenomenon than there are examples of it because these strictures reduce the number of relevant cases to a mere handful. In such investigations it is impossible to adjudicate among competing explanations. In the language of the statistical method, the use of societies in explanatory statements often presents serious degrees-of-freedom problems, for the number of relevant explanatory variables may far exceed the number of cases. From the perspective of main-

stream social science, therefore, comparative social science is severely deficient in the opportunities it presents for testing theory.

But many comparativists, especially those who are qualitatively oriented,
are not often involved in "testing" theories per se. Rather, they *apply* theory
to cases in order to interpret them. Because the explanatory statements of
comparative social science cite attributes of macrosocial units, objects with
known identities and histories figure prominently in the conduct of inquiry.
Thus, it is very difficult to treat these units simply as the undifferentiated
raw material of empirical social science. There is an ever present pressure to
take into account and to explain the particularity of specific cases, which in
turn requires the use of case-oriented methods sensitive to time, place,
agency, and process.

Recall also that one of the distinctive goals of comparative social science is
to interpret significant historical outcomes. From the perspective of mainstream social science this goal imposes very restrictive boundaries on social
research, dramatically reducing the number of relevant observations. In essence, when a comparativist interprets significant historical outcomes, he or
she selects extreme values on a more general dependent variable (for instance, social revolution is an extreme value on a general measure of social
turmoil) and studies the cases with these extreme values exclusively. This
practice is justified by the qualitative break that exists between extreme values and lesser values on what might be viewed by some as a continuum and
also by the cultural importance and historical significance of these extreme
cases. Thus, the problem of having too few societies on which to test theory
is compounded by the fact that the interests and goals of comparative social
science (and scientists) often dictate the design of studies with a small number of cases—too few to permit the application of any technique of statistical
comparison.

Most comparativists, in fact, are interested in questions that are limited,
substantively and historically. The questions they ask usually are much
more circumscribed than the abstract research question posed above concerning the effect of industrialization on the strength of the relationship between social class and party preference. In the typical comparative study,
only a small set of cases may provide the basis for empirical generalization.
Instances of social revolution, at least as defined by Skocpol (1979), for example, are few. There are also only a few instances of successful anti-
neocolonial revolt. There are more cases of dependent industrial development in the Third World today, but not so many that they can be studied

easily with quantitative cross-national techniques. Yet these and related topics demand the attention of comparative social scientists. The fact that there are few relevant instances of each phenomenon and that these instances have known identities and histories (that is, known particularity) has a powerful impact on the character of the research process.

ENTER THE COMPARATIVE METHOD

As the number of relevant observations decreases, the possibility of subjecting arguments to rigorous statistical testing diminishes. Other methods must be used. Smelser (1976 : 157) argues that the method of "systematic comparative illustration" (a method he portrays as a crude approximation of more sophisticated statistical methods) must be used when the number of relevant cases is small: "This method is most often required in the comparative analysis of national units or cultures." Smelser provides as one example of the method of systematic comparative illustration Tocqueville's three-way comparison of American, French, and English customs. Tocqueville argued simply that the conditions these collectivities share (such as language in the case of the English and the Americans) could not be used to explain their differences and that differences could not be used to explain similarities (Smelser 1976 : 158). In general, the technique of systematic comparative illustration involves applications of Mill's (1843) method of agreement and his indirect method of difference. (These case-oriented techniques are discussed in detail in Chapter 3.)

In an earlier work, Smelser (1973) called this systematic analysis of similarities and differences the comparative method and contrasted it with the statistical method. In his more recent *Comparative Methods in the Social Sciences* (1976), however, Smelser argues that, broadly speaking, virtually all social scientific methods are comparative and that the method of systematic comparative illustration is inferior to the statistical method as a comparative method. It is inferior, according to Smelser, because it must be used when the number of relevant cases is small and the possibility of establishing systematic control over the sources of variation in social phenomena is reduced. The possibilities for social scientific generalization are reduced.

In fact, the method that Smelser calls "the method of systematic comparative illustration" is what social scientists traditionally have called the comparative method. It forms the core of the case-oriented strategy and is quite different from correlational methods which form the core of the variable-oriented strategy (see Chapters 3 and 4). It is proper to call this method the comparative method because it follows directly from asking questions about empirically defined, historically concrete, large-scale social entities and processes—the kinds of questions that comparative social scientists tend to ask. Questions that necessarily lead to detailed analyses of relatively small numbers of cases are asked in other types of social science, as well, but this type of investigation is most common in comparative social science.

Once it is admitted that the comparative method derives its distinctiveness from the special goals of comparative social science and that it is most often a direct consequence of engaging in this enterprise, the special features of the comparative method can be delineated.

THE LOGIC OF THE COMPARATIVE METHOD

"It is surprising, for all that has been said about the value of comparison, that a rigorous comparative methodology has not emerged. The reason for this lack may be the great difficulties that a rigorous comparative methodology would impose" (Porter 1970 : 144). Smelser might argue that a rigorous comparative method is a contradiction in terms because, by definition, the comparative method is used only when the number of relevant cases is too small to allow the investigator to establish statistical control over the conditions and causes of variation in social phenomena. While the number of cases relevant to an analysis certainly imposes constraints on rigor, often it is the combinatorial nature of the explanations of comparative social science and the holistic character of the comparative method that militate against this kind of rigor.

Most comparativists, especially those who are qualitatively oriented, are interested in specific historical sequences or outcomes and their causes across a set of similar cases. Historical outcomes often require complex, combinatorial explanations, and such explanations are very difficult to prove in a manner consistent with the norms of mainstream quantitative social science. When causal arguments are combinatorial, it is not the number of cases but their *limited variety* that imposes constraints on rigor.

When qualitatively oriented comparativists compare, they study how different conditions or causes fit together in one setting and contrast that with how they fit together in another setting (or with how they might fit together in some ideal-typic setting). That is, they tend to analyze each observational entity as an interpretable combination of parts—as a whole. Thus, the explanations of comparative social science typically cite convergent causal conditions, causes that fit together or combine in a certain manner.

A simple example illustrates this practice. A comparativist might argue that social class and party preference are strongly related to each other in a sample of British voters not *simply* because Great Britain is an industrial society but also because it has a long history of class mobilization and conflict which coincided with the development of its current political system. In effect, this explanation cites three convergent conditions: (1) a history of class struggle (2) coinciding with polity maturation (3) in a country that has been industrialized for a long time. It is their combined effect that explains the enduring individual-level relationship between social class and party preference. The argument would be that this configuration of causes explains the observed association.

To evaluate this argument rigorously, it would be necessary to find instances (among democratic countries) of all the logically possible combinations of the three conditions and then to assess the relationship between social class and party preference in each combination. Each logically possible combination should be examined because the argument is that it is the coincidence of these three conditions that explains the association. If the expected relationship is obtained only when these three conditions coincide, and if all instances of such concurrence manifest the predicted relationship, then the general statement would be supported.

It would be difficult to evaluate this argument because instances of all logically possible combinations of conditions are not available. A completely rigorous assessment would require the identification of democratic countries with eight different combinations of characteristics. (There are eight different logically possible combinations of three dichotomies.) Each different combination is conceived as a different situation, a different totality, not simply as a different collection of values on three variables. Some of these combinations, however, while logically possible, do not exist. At best, the investigator would be able to examine the combinations that do exist and assess the relationship between class and party within each of these configurations.

While this simple example shows the limitations placed on the comparative method as a consequence of its holistic nature, it also illustrates key features of the method. As already noted, the comparative method attends to configurations of conditions; it is used to determine the different combinations of conditions associated with specific outcomes or processes. Moreover, the comparative method is based on "logical methods" (see Gee 1950); it uses two of Mill's methods of inductive inquiry: the method of agreement and the indirect method of difference (Mill 1843; see also Skocpol 1979 : 36; Skocpol and Somers 1980; Zelditch 1971; Ragin and Zaret 1983). These methods use all available and pertinent data concerning the preconditions of a specific outcome and, by examining the similarities and differences among relevant instances, elucidate its causes.

Because the comparative method has this character, statistical criteria are less important to this approach. This means that the comparative method does not work with samples or populations but with all relevant instances of the phenomenon of interest and, further, that the explanations which result from applications of the comparative method are not conceived in probabilistic terms because every instance of a phenomenon is examined and accounted for if possible. Consequently, the comparative method is relatively insensitive to the relative frequency of different types of cases. For example, if there are many instances of a certain phenomenon and two combinations of conditions that produce it, both combinations are considered equally valid accounts of the phenomenon regardless of their relative frequency. If one is relatively infrequent, an application of the statistical method to this same set of data might obscure its existence. The comparative method would consider both configurations of conditions relevant since both result in the phenomenon of interest.

Smelser's argument implies that the comparative method is inferior to the statistical method. Is it? The comparative method is superior to the statistical method in several important respects. First, the statistical method is not combinatorial; each relevant condition typically is examined in a piecemeal manner. Thus, for example, the statistical method can answer the question: what is the effect of having a history of class struggle net of the effect of industrialization? But it is difficult to use this method to address questions concerning the consequences of different combinations of conditions (that is, to investigate situations as wholes). To investigate combinations of conditions, the user of the statistical method must examine statistical interactions. The examination of a large number of statistical interactions in variable-oriented studies is complicated by collinearity and by problems with scarce degrees of freedom, especially in comparative research where the number of relevant cases is often small. An exhaustive examination of different combinations of seven preconditions, for example, would require a statistical analysis of the effects of more than one hundred different interaction terms.

Second, applications of the comparative method produce explanations that account for every instance of a certain phenomenon. True, these explanations may contain interpretive accounts of the particularity of one or more deviating cases, but at least the comparative method automatically highlights these irregularities and requires the investigator to propose explanations of them. This concern makes the comparative method more consistent with the goal of interpreting specific cases and addressing historical specificity. This feature of the comparative method also makes it especially well suited for the task of building new theories and synthesizing existing theories.

Third, the comparative method does not require the investigator to pretend that he or she has a sample of societies drawn from a particular population so that tests of statistical significance can be used. The boundaries of a comparative examination are set by the investigator (see Walton 1973 : 174–175); they are not coterminous with the boundaries of an arbitrarily defined or (more typically) undefined population of societies or points in time or events in societies.

Finally, the comparative method forces the investigator to become familiar with the cases relevant to the analysis. To make meaningful comparisons of cases as wholes, the investigator must examine each case directly and compare each case with all other relevant cases. The statistical method, by contrast, requires the investigator only to disaggregate cases into variables and then to examine relationships among variables, not to conduct a direct examination of the differences and similarities among cases considered as configurations of characteristics (that is, as meaningful wholes).

In short, the comparative method is not a bastard cousin of the statistical method. It is qualitatively different from the statistical method, and it is uniquely suited to the kinds of questions that many comparativists ask.

THE QUALITATIVE/QUANTITATIVE SPLIT IN COMPARATIVE SOCIAL SCIENCE

As outlined here, the comparative method is essentially a case-oriented strategy of comparative research (see Chapter 3). The focus is on comparing cases, and cases are examined as wholes—as combinations of characteristics (Ragin and Zaret 1983). This orientation distinguishes it from mainstream statistical methodology. Of course, not all social scientists who call themselves comparativists use the comparative method as presented in this chapter. Many use a variable-oriented strategy which conforms to the methodological norms of mainstream social science with its emphasis on variables and their interrelationships. The usual goal of variable-oriented investigations is to produce generalizations about relationships among variables, not to understand or interpret specific historical outcomes in a small number of cases or in an empirically defined set of cases (see Chapter 4). Combined strategies also exist, but close examination usually shows that studies using combined strategies tend to fall into one of the two camps (see Chapter 5). Examples of combined strategies include variable-oriented analyses supplemented with case studies (as in Paige 1975 and Stephens 1979) and case studies reinforced with quantitative analyses (as in Shorter and Tilly 1974).

The dichotomized nature of comparative work (case-oriented comparative study versus variable-oriented analysis) makes it an ideal setting for examining methodological issues—especially the gap between qualitative and quantitative orientations and how this gap might be bridged. Comparative work is the one branch of contemporary American social science that accords high status to the qualitative analysis of a small number of cases. In comparative social science, the variable-oriented strategy poses a challenge to traditional qualitative approaches. In other social science research areas, by contrast, the opposite is true. Thus, in comparative social science there is an established case-oriented tradition that can be directly contrasted with a growing variable-oriented tradition.

In comparative social science the qualitative tradition is strong because other methodological divisions coincide with the qualitative/quantitative split. As the preceding discussion of the logic of the comparative method shows, qualitative researchers tend to ask historically and empirically defined questions and typically answer these questions historically, in terms of origins. Thus, qualitative comparative researchers are both holistic and interpretive in their approach to comparative materials.

The split between qualitative and quantitative work in comparative social science is further aggravated by the fact that all comparativists are concerned with questions of direct relevance to macrosocial units with meaningful social identities (nation-states, for example). These identities are crucial to qualitative researchers, whereas they sometimes confound the work of those who do quantitative cross-national work. (For example, Kuwait is always a troublesome outlier in studies of economic dependence and development.) This aspect of comparative social science magnifies its value as an arena for addressing methodological issues. Contrasts between research strategies are exaggerated and the (often political) implications of methodological decisions are readily apparent.

Development, for example, is an outcome that has attracted the attention of social scientists for some time. Yet it can be defined in a variety of ways. To define it in terms of gross national product per capita makes Western Europe, the United States, and a few oil-rich countries appear to be the most developed. Defining it in terms of satisfaction of basic human needs, however, shuffles the development hierarchy and Eastern European countries occupy more of the prominent positions. Alternatively, development can be defined politically and qualitatively in terms of the emergence of a national political culture supported by a stable central government which, in turn, is acknowledged as legitimate by its subjects. This third definition reshuffles the hierarchy (Mexico, for example, is among the more advanced countries according to this definition) and suggests a complete rethinking of issues surrounding the causes of development.

Thus, methodological decisions that might seem minor in other research areas have unavoidably political implications in comparative work. These implications are especially salient to researchers who do qualitative work.

LOOKING AHEAD

Before contrasting the two major strategies of comparative research (in Chapters 3 and 4), I address the issues of heterogeneity and causal complexity, especially multiple conjunctural causation, in Chapter 2. The latter issue is important for two reasons. First, many comparativists are especially interested in historical outcomes, and their explanations often cite combinations of causal conditions. The assessment of causal complexity, therefore, is of major importance to comparative social science. Second, the two major research strategies differ dramatically in their approach to causation. In the case-oriented approach, causal complexity is easier to examine (and to assert) because usually only a small number of cases are examined. In the variable-oriented approach, by contrast, causal complexity poses difficult specification issues. Thus, the examination of causal complexity provides an important backdrop for contrasting the two major strategies.

2

Heterogeneity and Causal Complexity

"Social phenomena are complex." As social scientists we often make this claim. Sometimes we offer it as justification for the slow rate of social scientific progress. According to our collective folklore there are many, many variables—too many to specify—affecting the phenomena that interest us. Consequently, our explanations are often inadequate. This folklore implies that social phenomena are inordinately complicated and that it is surprising that anyone knows anything about social life.

Yet this depiction of social life does not fit well with experience. We sense that there is a great deal of order to social phenomena—that there is method to the madness. In fact, it is our strong sense that social phenomena are highly ordered that keeps us going. What is frustrating is the gulf that exists between this sense that the complexities of social phenomena can be unraveled and the frequent failures of our attempts to do so. The complaint that social phenomena are complex is not so much an excuse as it is an expression of this frustration.

This sense of order-in-complexity is very strong in comparative social science because it is not difficult to make sense of an individual case (say, a general strike) or to draw a few rough parallels across a range of cases (a number of general strikes separated in time and space). The challenge comes in trying to make sense of the diversity across cases in a way that unites similarities and differences in a single, coherent framework. In other words, it is often impossible to summarize in a theoretically or substantively meaningful way the order that seems apparent across diverse cases.

The problem of identifying order-in-complexity has two general forms.

One is the identification of types of cases—the problem of constructing useful empirical typologies. Most Third World countries are economically dependent on the developed capitalist countries, for example, but in different ways (see Cardoso 1973, 1977). What are the characteristic forms of dependency? How many different forms are there? Such empirical typologies are important because they set boundaries on comparability. It would be unreasonable, for example, to expect a certain change in the world economy to have identical consequences in different types of dependent countries.

The other characteristic form of the problem of order-in-complexity concerns the difficulty involved in assessing causal complexity, especially multiple conjunctural causation. When an outcome results from several different combinations of conditions, it is not easy to identify the decisive causal combinations across a range of cases, especially when the patterns are confounded. Many different combinations of conditions, for example, may cause the leaders of a government to resign ("regime failure"). These combinations may vary both within and between countries. Yet there is certainly a describable order to these combinations, a patterning that is comprehensible, identifiable, and possibly predictive as well.

Though very different conceptually, these two characteristic forms of the problem of order-in-complexity parallel each other. The first concerns simplifying the complexity among combinations of characteristics of cases and then constructing a model of the types that exist. The second concerns simplifying the complexity among combinations of causes of an outcome (observable across a range of cases) and then constructing a model of these causal combinations. Because the two characteristic forms of the problem are parallel, I focus the discussion in this chapter on only one—the problem of deciphering causal complexity (especially multiple conjunctural causation). This problem has a definite advantage over the first because it is relevant to the general concern in social science for causation, which, in turn, is central to explanation. Parallels between the two problems are examined in later chapters, where I show that the solutions to these two problems provide complementary approaches to the general problem of deciphering order-in-complexity. I begin by discussing the relation between interests and complexity and then address the issue of causal complexity specifically.

INTERESTS, SIMPLICITY, AND COMPLEXITY

Whether any aspect of social life or social organization is simple or complex depends ultimately on the interests of social scientists (and, by implication, the interests of their audiences). For example, it may be true in a probabilistic sense that children of divorced parents are more likely to drop out of school. This is a perfectly acceptable empirical generalization which presents one aspect of social life in a simple and straightforward manner. It may be entirely unsatisfactory, however, to an investigator (or school principal) interested in understanding how, from the perspective of dropouts, events seem to conspire to force them to quit school. Broken homes may be part of the general context for some of these (apparently) conspiring circumstances, but only a small part. The simple probabilistic relation between broken homes and dropping out is only one of several starting points for a more thorough investigation.

Another simple example comes from the study of face-to-face interaction. Certain patterns of interaction in dyads (asking more questions, for example) are related to the distribution of power. This is a straightforward generalization from empirical data. The fact that this simple, probabilistic relationship exists does not mean, however, that it is pointless to study the variety of situations in which the relation is reversed (with the more powerful person in the dyad displaying an interaction style usually characteristic of less powerful individuals) or to try to generalize about these exceptions. The fact that a general pattern exists does not negate the value of trying to unravel the intricacies of situations in which the relationship is reversed.

The direct relation between interests and the degree of complexity of social phenomena is even more apparent in comparative social science. Several macrosocial theories, for example, argue that international inequality is maintained, in part, by the economic dependence of underdeveloped countries on developed countries. Drawing on these theories, a number of researchers have documented a weak but consistently negative cross-national relationship between economic dependence (such as degree of specialization in the export of primary commodities) and economic growth (rate of increase in GNP per capita). Thus, interest in a global argument about international inequality has inspired general tests of the relationship, and a simple cross-national pattern has been confirmed, though not overwhelmingly. (See Bornschier and others 1978 and Rubinson and Holtzman 1981.)

Other perspectives argue, however, that dependency and GNP per capita growth are not necessarily incompatible and that several countries have experienced "associated-dependent development" (Cardoso 1973). Note that this perspective is more an elaboration of the first (which argues, in effect, that dependency uniformly stunts economic development) than a rejection. The second argues that dependency and growth are compatible in a context of severe (and possibly increasing) internal inequality and regime repressiveness (see Bradshaw 1985). Several studies have documented cases of associated-dependent development and have shown that it forms a complex of traits consistent with theoretical expectations (see Evans 1979). In this second line of research, detailed study at the case level was mandated because the goal was to document associated-dependent development as a relatively complex totality in the modest number of cases where it has occurred.

The contrast between these two schools of thought and the picture they present of the relation between interests and complexity is clear. The first line of research, which dictates relatively little concern for complexity, views underdeveloped countries as a more or less homogeneous mass and applies a single, variable-oriented causal model to the entire population with some success. The second line of research, by contrast, dictates greater concern for complexity and views the underdeveloped world as heterogeneous—a set containing several distinct populations. Neither view is incorrect. Ultimately, the degree to which a set of observations or cases is one population or many depends on the interests of the investigator and those of the intended audience.

The close connection between interests and complexity in comparative research is also evident in many comparativists' predilection for studying cases that register "extreme values" on important dimensions of cross-national variation. Comparativists often argue that cases with extreme values are qualitatively different from other cases and that this quality justifies close attention to their complexity, despite their relative infrequency. The example of countries experiencing social revolutions versus countries experiencing milder forms of social turmoil is useful here. (The argument applies equally well to other infrequent but important large-scale social phenomena.) The fact that some elements of a revolution are present—albeit in muted form—in nonrevolutionary cases does not change the fact that a social revolution is an unusual combination of circumstances. In disaggregated form, the different components of a revolution (which might be present in different countries at different times—for example, executive instability in the United States during the Watergate period) are not revolutionary because it is the *whole* these components form when combined that gives them their revolutionary character. The fact that a few superficial commonalities exist across revolutionary and nonrevolutionary cases does not detract from the importance of social revolution as a theoretical category with considerable cultural and political significance—a phenomenon demanding the special attention of social scientists.

Some comparativists argue further that cases registering extreme values deserve detailed attention because they provide especially pure examples of certain social phenomena. (See, for instance, Durkheim in *Elementary Forms of the Religious Life*.) Dumont (1970), for example, argues that the Indian caste system provides a unique opportunity to study human social stratification in its purest known form. Anthropologists (such as Harris 1978 and 1985) frequently justify their selection of cases on these grounds, usually with the goal of showing that emergent cultural patterns that may seem bizarre or extreme in some way have important practical value and should therefore be understood in a larger context.

In general, attention to complexity is justified whenever it is argued that a certain historical outcome (say, the Sandinista Revolution in Nicaragua) or set of similar outcomes (say, anti-neocolonial revolutions) is historically or culturally significant in its own right and therefore demanding of social scientific interpretation. The interpretation of important historical events and outcomes (which includes a wide array of macrosocial phenomena ranging from brief episodes of collective action to the rise of the West) is one of the defining features of comparative social science—one of its special missions. Furthermore, this type of interpretation is a primary avenue for the dissemination of social scientific knowledge. While general statements about major dimensions of macrosocial variation and their interrelation (that is, the stuff of variable-oriented comparative social science) are important, the reach of these general statements beyond a purely academic audience is limited by their abstract character (see Ragin 1985).

Interest in complexity is most apparent whenever comparative social scientists address specific historical outcomes, especially when they examine the causes of similar outcomes in different contexts. It is difficult to specify historical causation across a range of cases, however, because such causation is often conjunctural. I turn now to a general discussion of the issue of multiple conjunctural causation as it relates to comparative research.

CAUSAL COMPLEXITY

Virtually all everyday events show causal complexity. A funny joke told in the wrong setting can fall flat. Some compliments come off like insults; some insults come off like jokes. Certain behavioral patterns in some individuals are seen as virtues; in others they are seen as vices. In all these examples context plays an important part. This is because human understanding of causation and of events in general is fundamentally holistic. (See

Nisbett and Ross 1980.) Parts are not viewed in isolation but in context of the whole they form. To change one or more elements often changes how the whole is perceived or understood, which, in turn, has an impact on the meaning of each individual part. (For a more sophisticated treatment of these and related issues, see Goffman 1974.)

Examples of causal complexity at the macrolevel abound. A president's popularity may increase as the result of military intervention in other areas of the world; it can also plummet. News about higher interest rates can cause the stock market to go up or down, depending on other economic news. Appeals to patriotic sentiment by political leaders are sometimes quite effective, depending on the timing and character of the appeal and the specific mix of national symbols used in the appeal. But they often fall flat. It is hazardous to predict when an appeal to patriotism will work. In short, the prediction of collective sentiments, mass behavior, and aggregate trends in general is a risky business. We are awash with political and economic advisors and consultants precisely because of the causal complexity of national-level events and processes.

Most national-level events of interest to comparativists show a great deal of causal complexity. Some polities in the Third World, for example, are thought to be stable because they are democratic (Costa Rica, for example), but others are thought to have failed because of the instability that was magnified by the adoption of democratic procedures (certain countries of sub-Saharan Africa, for instance). The specific contribution of democracy to political stability depends on context. Another example: sometimes a prolonged deterioration in socioeconomic conditions demoralizes people and makes them apathetic (see Gurr 1970). In other circumstances it may make them revolutionary (see Walton 1984). Still, there are instances of mass mobilization occurring in the absence of important socioeconomic change. Another example: in some countries ethnic inequality fuels ethnic political mobilization (as in Wales), while in others there is ethnic political mobilization without dramatic ethnic inequality (as in Belgium). Ethnic political mobilization can result from a variety of seemingly unrelated causes. There is no universal explanation of this or most other large-scale events common to contemporary nation-states.

Whenever social scientists examine large-scale change (such as the collapse of a polity, the emergence of an ethnic political party, or the rapid decline in support for a regime), they find that it is usually *combinations* of conditions that produce change. This is not the same as arguing that change results from many variables, as in the statement "both X_1 and X_2 affect Y," because this latter type of argument asserts that change in either causal variable produces a change in Y, the dependent variable.

When a causal argument cites a combination of conditions, it is concerned with their intersection. It is the intersection of a set of conditions in time and in space that produces many of the large-scale qualitative changes, as well as many of the small-scale events, that interest social scientists, not the separate or independent effects of these conditions. Such processes exhibit what John Stuart Mill (1843) called "chemical causation." The basic idea is that a phenomenon or a change emerges from the intersection of appropriate preconditions—the right ingredients for change. In the absence of any one of the essential ingredients, the phenomenon—or the change—does not emerge. This conjunctural or combinatorial nature is a key feature of causal complexity.

The conjunctural nature of social causation is not the only property of social phenomena that makes them complex. Typically, there are several combinations of conditions that may produce the same emergent phenomenon or the same change. The comparison of many large-scale changes, for example, often leads to the conclusion that for a given type of outcome (say, the formation of regionally based ethnic political parties) there are many causally relevant intersections of conditions. In one set of cases, for example, a coincidence of ethnic inequality, a high degree of government centralization, and increased domination of regional economies by multinational firms may explain the emergence of ethnic parties. In another set, a coincidence of ethnic equality, decentralized government, and an increased migration of members of the numerically dominant ethnic group into regions containing minority ethnic groups might explain the formation of ethnic parties. In the first set, it is the lure of separatism that spurs ethnic mobilization. In the second, it is the infringement by the majority group on formerly ethnic turf that stimulates ethnic mobilization. These two combinations of conditions certainly would not exhaust all instances of regionally based ethnic political mobilization. Other combinations might be identified, and the specification of other causal combinations might further the identification of different types of ethnic mobilization. The point is not the number of causal combinations or types but the fact that the same general outcome—ethnic political mobilization—may result from various combinations of causes.

That social causation is often both multiple and conjunctural is consistent with commonsense notions about how the world works. The key consideration is the whole—how different conditions or parts fit together. The problem that social scientists face is to unravel the empirically relevant causal combinations. In other words, once the possibility of multiple conjunctural causation is admitted, it is necessary to determine how different conditions fit together—and in how many different combinations—to produce a given outcome. The identification and interpretation of these causal configurations (or causal complexes) allows the investigator to delineate the different empirical processes and causal mechanisms relevant to a specific outcome.

Thus, social phenomena are complex and difficult to unravel not because there are too many variables affecting them, although the number of causal variables is certainly important, but because different causally relevant conditions can combine in a variety of ways to produce a given outcome. In short, it is the combinatorial, and often complexly combinatorial, nature of social causation that makes the problem of identifying order-in-complexity demanding.

THE ANALYSIS OF CAUSAL COMPLEXITY

Causal complexity is not easily unraveled, paradoxically, because of the relatively limited diversity of empirical social phenomena. The similarities and differences among nonexperimental cases confound attempts to specify social causation unambiguously. If social scientists could create social phenomena displaying all the different combinations of causal conditions and then observe outcomes (that is, if they could conduct experiments), it would be a simple matter to explicate the decisive causal combinations. Obviously, this is not possible, so they have developed research strategies appropriate for nonexperimental data. Before addressing nonexperimental strategies, I examine the experimental design standard that inspires nonexperimental approaches.

The ideal social scientific comparison is identical in structure to the simple experiment. In a simple experiment an investigator compares an experimental group, which has been subjected to an experimental treatment, with a control group, which differs from the experimental group in only one respect—it does not receive the treatment. Only one factor, the treatment, is allowed to vary; all other conditions are held constant or randomized. If significant posttreatment differences between the experimental and control group emerge, these differences are credited to the experimental or treatment variable, and a tentative cause–effect sequence is established.

Experimental design has an unrivaled directness and simplicity, and it is immune to some of the inferential errors that affect other methods. Of course, experimental research is confronted with a host of threats to its validity (see Campbell and Stanley 1966; Cook and Campbell 1979), but it is more capable of deciphering causal complexity than other techniques. This is because it allows the investigator to manipulate causes directly—to manufacture a basis for making comparisons.

Many features of social life confound attempts to unravel causal complexity when experimental methods cannot be used. Three are especially relevant to this discussion because they concern issues of multiple and conjunctural causation. First, rarely does an outcome of interest to social scientists have a single cause. The conditions conducive to strikes, for example, are many; there is no single condition that is universally capable of causing a strike. Second, causes rarely operate in isolation. Usually, it is the combined effect of various conditions, their intersection in time and space, that produces a certain outcome. Thus, social causation is often both multiple and conjunctural, involving different combinations of causal conditions. Third, a specific cause may have opposite effects depending on context. For example, changes in living conditions may increase or decrease the probability of strikes, depending on other social and political conditions (Snyder 1975). The fact that some conditions have contradictory effects depending on context further complicates the identification of empirical regularities because it may appear that a condition is irrelevant when in fact it is an essential part of several causal combinations in both its presence and absence state.

Natural scientists attempt to establish causes that are either necessary or sufficient or both necessary and sufficient. In situations where causation is multiple and conjunctural, there may be no necessary or sufficient conditions for an outcome of interest. For example, if outcome Y occurs following the combination of X_1 and X_2 or the combination of X_3 and X_4, then none of the single conditions, X_1 through X_4, is either necessary or sufficient to produce Y. This possibility complicates the observation of causal relations in nonexperimental settings because investigators typically are not able to observe all logical combinations of the relevant causal conditions. Yet comparative social scientists are often confronted with phenomena that display this type of causation.

Multiple conjunctural causation can be assessed directly only in experimental designs. Suppose a researcher believes that three factors (X_1, X_2, and X_3) are causally relevant to Y and has strong reason to suspect that different

TABLE 1: Experimental Design Exhausting Logically Possible
Combinations of Three Treatments

	Treatments		
	x_1	x_2	x_3
Group 1:	absent	absent	absent
Group 2:	present	absent	absent
Group 3:	absent	present	absent
*Group 4:	present	present	absent
Group 5:	absent	absent	present
Group 6:	present	absent	present
*Group 7:	absent	present	present
Group 8:	present	present	present

*Groups showing change in outcome variable (y).

combinations of these factors cause Y. The presence of any one factor alone is not thought to be sufficient; only certain (as yet unspecified) combinations of factors are capable of causing Y. Determining the relevant combinations of conditions is a simple matter if an experimental design is feasible. In this example the experimenter would set up eight different experimental groups and apply different combinations of the treatment variables, as shown in Table 1. The investigator would examine Y under each of the eight conditions to see which combinations of X's cause Y. If Y were to occur only in groups 4 and 7, for example, the investigator would conclude that if X_2 is accompanied by X_1 or X_3, but not by both, then Y will result. (In this example, X_2 is a necessary but not a sufficient condition for Y.)

The beauty of experimental design is that it is a simple matter to examine combinations of conditions and determine the specific combinations that are causally relevant. Thus, causal complexity, which is a key characteristic of social life, is unraveled. Decisive comparisons can be made because all the relevant combinations of conditions are manufactured by the investigator. In the hypothetical study described here, Y is caused by X_2 when it is combined with either X_1 or X_3, but not when it is combined with both. There are three decisive comparisons that establish this finding: the comparison of group 4 with groups 2 and 3, which establishes that X_2 and X_1 must be combined to produce Y; the comparison of group 7 with groups 3 and 5, which establishes that X_2 and X_3 must be combined to produce Y; and the comparison of groups 4 and 7 with group 8, which establishes that when X_2 is combined with both X_1 and X_3, then Y does not result. (Other comparisons are also important, but these are the most decisive.) In each of the key comparisons an experimental group is compared with other groups differing in only one causally relevant condition.

Of course, social scientists rarely ask questions that can be addressed with experimental methods. Their questions are usually shaped by the events around them, and social scientists often are called upon to interpret events (or simply desire to do so), including the social and historical forces that have shaped contemporary social arrangements. For example, some social scientists are interested in the conditions that lead to different types of collective action. What conditions cause peasants to rebel? What conditions cause workers to go on strike? What conditions cause citizens to feel nationalistic or cause members of an ethnic minority to organize ethnic political parties? Obviously, experimental methods are not applicable to these questions. It is impossible to manipulate conditions affecting large masses of people, and social scientists must be content to study naturally occurring (that is, "non-experimental") data. Yet there is good reason to believe that the causes of these phenomena are both multiple and conjunctural and therefore require experiment-like analyses. Only when naturally occurring data approximate experimental designs is it possible to decipher the order-in-complexity that seems apparent in these phenomena.

Consider, for example, the following hypothetical examination of the causes of peasant revolts in different areas within a single country. Assume there are four causes to consider across six different regions, with different combinations of causes appearing as in Table 2.

There are no experiment-like contrasts among the six regions because all pairs of regions differ on at least two of the four causes. When this pattern exists, it is difficult to draw any strong conclusion. For example, data from regions 3 and 6 indicate that land hunger combined with an absence of commercialization of agriculture may be important to peasant revolts. But region 4 had the opposite pattern on these two variables and also experienced a revolt. Regions 3 and 4 both combine peasant communalism and few middle peasants, suggesting that peasant revolts are more likely in traditional peasant communities lacking an upwardly mobile class of middle peasants. But region 6 has the opposite values on these two variables and experienced a revolt. Examination of the four regions with revolts suggests that if any two of four conditions are present, then a peasant revolt is likely. But region 2

TABLE 2: Hypothetical Regional Data Showing Distribution of
Causes of Peasant Revolts

Region	Revolt	L	C	P	M
1	no	no	no	no	no
2	no	yes	yes	yes	yes
3	yes	yes	no	yes	no
4	yes	no	yes	yes	no
5	yes	yes	yes	no	no
6	yes	yes	no	no	yes

L = Land hunger
C = Commercialization of agriculture
P = Peasant communalism
M = Middle peasants

had all four conditions present, and a revolt failed to occur. In short, it would be unwise to draw any strong conclusions from these data. The diversity of causal patterns among these cases is too limited to permit sound conclusions based on the data.

CURRENT ALTERNATIVES TO EXPERIMENTAL DESIGN

The observations offered above concerning the limited applicability of experimental designs to most social science data are certainly not new. The discussion serves primarily to establish what most American-trained social scientists, both comparativists and noncomparativists, consider to be the ultimate standard in social science methodology: the precision and causal certainty of experimental design. (See also Lieberson 1985.) Social scientific statements about empirical phenomena are thought to be sound to the extent that the demands of experimental design (which could be considered a methodological ideal type) have been met. The closer the approximation to the type of comparison fundamental to experimental design, the more sound the statement of empirical regularity.

Obviously, social scientists rarely come close, and some argue that social scientists should simply acknowledge the limitations of their efforts and give up the experimental design standard. While it might be possible to abandon the standard, comparison still provides the primary basis for empirical generalization. As Swanson (1971 : 145) notes, "thinking without comparison is unthinkable"—and comparison, at its social scientific best, involves experiment-like contrasts. Is it possible to ask the questions that social scientists ask and still retain experiment-like comparison as an ideal? There have been two basic responses to this question. Each response constitutes a research strategy; both research strategies have long histories.

The first strategy has been for comparatively oriented social scientists to use case-oriented methods, also known as *the* comparative method (see Chapters 1 and 3; Smelser 1973; Ragin 1983), qualitative historical methods (Ragin and Zaret 1983), the method of systematic comparative illustration (Smelser 1976), and logical methods (Gee 1950; see also Skocpol and Somers 1980), to name only a few of the many labels that have been applied. Investigators who use this strategy usually work only with small, theoretically defined sets of cases, and they compare cases with each other as wholes to arrive at modest generalizations, usually about historical origins and outcomes, concerning relatively narrow classes of phenomena.

Some have argued that this tradition follows in the footsteps of Weber, and German historiography more generally, and that it is primarily an interpretive tradition. While there is a good deal of truth to the claim that the tradition is Weberian (Ragin and Zaret 1983), this strategy is usually not merely interpretive but also causal-analytic. To characterize this tradition as predominantly interpretive implies that the experimental design standard is irrelevant—that a concern for historical essences and particularities removes any need for experiment-like comparisons.

Considering only extreme examples of case-oriented investigation, it is true that this type of inquiry often involves a different way of seeing social phenomena. The best work in this tradition, however, the work that is most relevant to the concerns of social scientists, does not stop with historical interpretation. Two tasks are usually apparent: interpreting historically significant or decisive social phenomena and determining the causes of important categories of social phenomena (such as the origins of different types of modernizing revolutions, as in Moore 1966).

The case-oriented strategy attempts to approximate experimental rigor by identifying comparable instances of a phenomenon of interest and then analyzing the theoretically important similarities and differences among them. This approach provides a basis for establishing modest empirical generalizations concerning historically defined categories of social phenomena. Of course, there is rarely a sufficient variety of cases to prove or disprove causal arguments. Typically, several possible explanations can be supported

in a given set of cases. The limited variety of cases imposes a necessary inde-
terminancy. Thus, the investigator must support his or her chosen explanation by citing surrounding circumstances and, more generally, by interpreting cases. This attention to the details of individual cases engenders a rich
research dialogue between the investigator and the evidence.

The second strategy also has deep intellectual roots, which can be traced
back to Comte and Durkheim (see Ragin and Zaret 1983), but it has recently
received a strong boost from mainstream social science methodology, especially quantitative methods. The second strategy typically is not concerned
with accounting for historically defined phenomena, such as modernizing
revolutions or peasant rebellions. It is concerned with formulating broad
generalizations about societies and other large-scale social organizations.
Unlike the first strategy, which is oriented toward explaining specific cases or
historically defined categories of social phenomena, the second strategy is
more concerned with variables and their relationships. Its primary goal is to
test abstract hypotheses derived from general theories concerning relationships between features of social units such as societies conceived as variables.

A preference for generality over specificity enhances the compatibility of
the second strategy with the goals of mainstream social science which, in
turn, has allowed the use of mainstream methods, especially techniques of
statistical control. This strategy attempts to approximate the rigor of experimental methods through statistical manipulation. The effects of competing
and confounding variables are "removed" or "partialed" in estimating the
effect of each variable. In this way conditions are "controlled," and a basis
for generalizing about confounded causes is manufactured mathematically.
(These procedures and the logic of statistical control in nonexperimental research in general are critically evaluated in Lieberson 1985.)

Note that in this strategy it is possible to manufacture a basis for generalizing about causes only by making simplifying assumptions about their
operation. These assumptions sometimes are not necessary, but they greatly
simplify the task of examining empirical data and the problem of summarizing and presenting the general patterns of covariation that exist among diverse cases. Statistical techniques are biased toward simplifying complexity
through assumptions because the assumptions are often built into the procedures themselves. Thus, these techniques do not decipher causal complexity
but eliminate perplexing elements of it.

A common (and sometimes testable) assumption, for example, is that
causes are additive. One problem with this assumption is that it asserts that

the effect of a cause is the same in all contexts—regardless of the values or levels of other causal variables. This assertion directly contradicts the idea, held dear by many case-oriented investigators, that causation, especially historical causation, is often multiple and conjunctural. (This issue is addressed in greater detail in Chapters 3 and 4.) Assumptions that are built into statistical models have a profound effect on the nature of the research dialogue—the interaction between the investigator and the evidence—that develops in the variable-oriented approach. The dialogue centers on the issue of specifying the "correct" model. The identity, diversity, and particularity of cases tend to be obscured.

In the next two chapters, I examine these broad strategies in detail. I pay special attention to the way scholars in both traditions have attempted to approximate features of experimental design. It is important to point out that in many respects I present exaggerated versions of these strategies and that many variants and combinations exist. In fact, the best comparative work usually combines these two strategies in some way (see Chapter 5). After all, for most comparativists the problem is not choosing strategies per se, but doing good comparative work. Following my presentation of the basics of these broad strategies, I discuss several ways these strategies have been combined. Finally, I present a middle road between the two which integrates important features of both. This integration is the foundation for my elaboration of Boolean techniques of qualitative comparison.

3

Case-Oriented Comparative Methods

Often, comparativists seek to formulate historical (or, in Nagel's 1961 terminology, "genetic") explanations of specific historical outcomes or historically defined categories of empirical phenomena. Instances of such phenomena are intrinsically interesting to comparativists as cases, in part because they embody certain values (Weber 1949, 1975, 1977) but also because they are finite and enumerable. It is their particularity—the fact that they are instances of significant events or phenomena—that attracts the attention of the investigator. Sometimes, there is only one or two or a small handful of such instances.

Various case-oriented research strategies have emerged to accommodate this interest in specific cases and specific historical chronologies. Present-day followers of Weber, for example, employ a comparative strategy centered on extensive use of ideal types and other theoretical devices to guide the interpretation of empirical cases (Bonnell 1980; Ragin and Zaret 1983). Others use comparative materials to conduct "parallel demonstrations of theory" or to analyze causal mechanisms across sets of comparable cases (Skocpol and Somers 1980). Still others use "universalizing," "encompassing," or "variation-finding" strategies (Tilly 1984) to aid comprehension of diverse historical trajectories. Most investigators who use case-oriented strategies, however, are not self-consciously methodological; that is, they do not regard the case-oriented strategies they use as formal methodologies. Nevertheless, there is substantial agreement among comparativists concerning the essential features of the case-oriented approach.

The goals of case-oriented investigation often are both historically interpretive and causally analytic. Interpretive work, as defined in Chapter 1, attempts to account for significant historical outcomes or sets of comparable
outcomes or processes by piecing evidence together in a manner sensitive to
historical chronology and offering limited historical generalizations which
are sensitive to context. Thus, comparativists who use case-oriented strategies often want to understand or interpret specific cases because of their in-
trinsic value. Most, but not all, case-oriented work is also causal-analytic.
This companion goal is to produce limited generalizations concerning the
causes of theoretically defined categories of empirical phenomena (such as
the emergence of class-based political parties) common to a set of cases.

In *Social Origins of Dictatorship and Democracy*, for example, Barrington Moore interprets the process of polity modernization in seven major
countries *and* pinpoints common historical features constituting three major
paths to polity modernization. While Moore's purpose is both to interpret
these cases and to pinpoint the historical origins of these different paths, the
goal of causal generalization is given precedence over the goal of historical
interpretation. In some investigations, however, the goal of interpretation
takes precedence over the goal of causal analysis. For example, while case-
oriented comparisons are very important in Bendix's work (1977, 1978), his
primary goal is to interpret each case. He produces little in the way of empirical generalization because he emphasizes the particularity of each case as
a representative of a distinct theoretical type. Thus, differences between the
cases he selects overwhelm their similarities.

Many empirically oriented comparativists (such as Smelser 1976; Skocpol and Somers 1980) stress the basic, underlying similarities between case-
oriented comparative work and other kinds of empirical social science. They
emphasize the use of empirical data on cases to decipher important causal
patterns and downplay the interpretive side of comparative work. The goal of
causal generalization is emphasized to create a gulf between comparative social science and highly abstract, nonempirical work that traditionally has
been called interpretive (that is, work which is concerned almost exclusively
with problems of meaning). There is no necessary contradiction, however,
between doing empirically based causal analysis and interpreting cases historically. Both goals (causal analysis and historical interpretation—as defined in this work) are important; having one does not entail a denial of the
other.

Regardless of which goal may take precedence, the underlying logic of case-oriented comparisons is roughly the same. Most discussions of case-oriented methods begin (and often end) with John Stuart Mill's presentation of canons of experimental inquiry in *A System of Logic: Ratiocinative and Inductive* (1843). Mill outlined several general research strategies for establishing empirical generalizations. His main goal was to establish a logical foundation for inductively oriented scientific investigation. Two of Mill's methods are of particular relevance to case-oriented investigations: the method of agreement and the indirect method of difference.

MILL'S METHOD OF AGREEMENT

The method of agreement is by far the simplest and the most straightforward of Mill's methods, but it is also generally regarded as an inferior technique that is likely to lead to faulty empirical generalizations. Simply stated, the method of agreement argues that if two or more instances of a phenomenon under investigation have only one of several possible causal circumstances in common, then the circumstance in which all the instances agree is the cause of the phenomenon of interest. The application of this method is straightforward: if an investigator wants to know the cause of a certain phenomenon, he or she should first identify instances of the phenomenon and then attempt to determine which circumstance invariably precedes its appearance. The circumstance that satisfies this requirement is the cause. Although Mill stated that researchers should look for a single causal condition in which all instances agree, he would probably allow for the possibility that this single circumstance might be a recurrent combination of conditions. All instances would have to agree in this single causal combination.

The method of agreement, especially in comparative social science, proceeds by elimination. Suppose, for example, that an investigator is interested in the causes of peasant revolts and gathers evidence on major revolts. Among the possible causes are land hunger (see Paige 1975), rapid commercialization of agriculture (see Wolf 1969; Moore 1966; Chirot and Ragin 1975), a strong middle peasantry (see Stinchcombe 1961; Wolf 1969), and peasant traditionalism (see Chirot and Ragin 1975; Moore 1966). Suppose further that all the possible causal circumstances exist in the first case the investigator examines. Which one is the cause? The method of agreement dictates that the researcher examine the other instances of peasant revolt in an effort to eliminate any of the four explanatory variables. For example, if an instance of peasant revolt in a country or region lacking a strong middle peasantry could be found, then this factor could be eliminated as a possible explanation of peasant revolts. The search for cases lacking one of the other four conditions would continue until no other cause could be eliminated. The remaining cause (or set of causes) would be considered decisive because at this point the investigator could conclude that all cases of peasant revolt agree in only this precondition (or set of preconditions). If all cases agreed on all four causes, then the investigator would conclude that all four conditions are important.

The method of agreement is used extensively by both comparativists and noncomparativists. Comparativists often use it when they are concerned primarily with a single case. To support their interpretation of a causal sequence in a specific case they often cite secondary cases that agree with the first in displaying both the cause and the effect. Many noncomparativists also use the method of agreement. It bears a striking resemblance, for example, to the technique of analytic induction used by many qualitatively oriented microsociologists. Analytic induction is useful both for eliminating causes, as in the work of Lindesmith (1968), and for demonstrating cause, as in Cressey's (1953) work.

Essentially, the method of agreement is a search for patterns of invariance. All instances of a phenomenon are identified, and the investigator attempts to determine which of the possible causal variables is constant across all instances. Thus, a constant (say, peasant revolt) is explained with another constant (say, rapid commercialization of agriculture—if all cases agreed on only this cause). Mill believed that the main problem with this method is its inability to establish any necessary link between cause and effect. For example, the fact that all instances of peasant revolt also display rapid commercialization of agriculture does not guarantee that rapid commercialization causes peasant revolts. Both rapid commercialization and peasant revolts may result from some unidentified third factor (say, a change in the political balance between the state and the landed aristocracy resulting from the increased power of large landowners) and the observed relationship may be spurious. Mill reasoned that the only way to be certain that a cause–effect sequence has been established is to attempt to recreate it experimentally.

There is another problem with the method of agreement that is particularly relevant to comparative social science: the method of agreement is completely incapacitated by multiple causation (which was known to Mill as plural causation). If peasant revolts result from *either* rapid commercialization *or* land hunger, then there may be instances where revolt has resulted from only rapid commercialization and other instances where revolt has resulted from only increased land hunger. Application of the method of agreement would lead to the incorrect conclusion that neither of these factors causes revolts. In situations of multiple causation, therefore, the method of agreement is likely to yield incorrect results. (Of course, it still might be possible to argue in advance that two causes are somehow equivalent at the conceptual level, and the presence of either constitutes a single, invariant cause. Mill did not address this issue directly because of his interest in techniques of inductive inquiry.)

Plural causation is an important problem because many comparative social scientists use a technique known as *paired comparisons* to support their arguments. Specifically, they compare pairs of cases to reject competing explanatory variables. The typical argument has the form, "Even though X (land hunger) appears to be the cause of Y (peasant revolt) in country A, it is not, because country B also has Y (peasant revolt) but does not have X (land hunger)." There is nothing inherently wrong with such statements if the phenomenon of interest is known to result from a single cause (which, of course, is impossible to know in advance). To allow the possibility of multiple causation, however, closes off paired comparisons as an avenue of argumentation and makes application of the method of agreement a relatively futile exercise.

Mill cautioned against liberal use of the method of agreement and suggested that investigators use experimental designs whenever possible (a technique he called the method of difference). Some (such as Skocpol 1979) have argued that Mill's method of difference, which involves comparisons of cases differing in only one causal condition, the treatment variable, is available to comparative social scientists in the form of longitudinal comparisons. Russia in 1905, for example, resembled Russia in 1917 in most respects. What key differences account for the greater success of the 1917 revolt? While longitudinal comparisons are often useful, they do not come close to conforming to the demands of experimental design. One obvious key difference between Russia in 1917 and Russia in 1905 is the simple fact that 1917 Russia had already experienced 1905 Russia, whereas 1905 Russia had not. (Other problems with this design are discussed in Campbell and Stanley 1966 and Cook and Campbell 1979.) Mill argued that when direct experimental manipulation is not feasible, investigators should use the indirect method of difference, a method which attempts to approximate experimental design with nonexperimental data.

Before describing the indirect method, it should be noted that the method of difference is available to investigators as a theoretical method (see Stinchcombe 1978; Bonnell 1980). It is possible to contrast an empirical case with an imaginary case representing a theoretically pure instance of the phenomenon of interest—that is, conduct a type of thought experiment (see Weber 1949 and 1978). For example, an investigator might contrast the Sandinista Revolution in Nicaragua with a theoretical pure instance of anti-neocolonial revolution (that is, with an ideal-typic anti-neocolonial revolt constructed from knowledge of many such cases and embellished with the aid of theory). The goal in this analysis would be to link the differences between the Nicaraguan case and the ideal-typic case in relevant causes to differences in outcomes. This method would allow the investigator to explain and interpret specific features of the Nicaraguan case. In this general type of analysis the divergence of the empirical case from the imaginary case in causes is the experimental or treatment variable; differences in outcome show the effect of the experimental variable (see Ragin 1985). While attractive, this method is a *theoretical* method and therefore not in the same class with such empirical methods as the method of agreement and the indirect method of difference.

MILL'S INDIRECT METHOD OF DIFFERENCE

Mill's indirect method of difference is a double application of the method of agreement. Suppose an investigator believes that rapid commercialization causes peasant revolts. First, the investigator identifies instances of peasant revolt to see if they agree in displaying rapid commercialization. If they do, then instances of the absence of peasant revolts (among peasant societies) are examined to see if they agree in displaying an absence of rapid commercialization. In effect, the presence and absence of peasant revolts is crosstabulated against the presence and absence of rapid commercialization in peasant societies. If all cases fall into the presence/presence or absence/absence cells of the 2 × 2 matrix, then the argument that rapid commercialization is the cause of peasant revolts is supported.

This pattern of results would correspond to a perfect zero-order correlation in statistical analysis, which also would support the inference of causation. Because of this correspondence, it is tempting to see the indirect method of difference as a simple statistical technique. After all, it involves cross-tabulations of causes and effects. It is not a statistical technique, however. Like the method of agreement, the indirect method of difference is used to establish patterns of invariance. Imperfect (that is, probabilistic) relationships are the province of statistical theory, not the indirect method of agreement. (In practice, of course, perfect relationships are rarely identified, and the investigator is forced to account for deviant cases.)

Ideally, Mill (1843) argues, the second set of cases—those displaying an absence of both the cause and the effect—should also provide a basis for rejecting competing hypotheses. Thus, for example, if the cases displaying both peasant revolts and rapid commercialization also display land hunger, a possible explanation of revolts, then some of the cases displaying an absence of both rapid commercialization and peasant revolts (ideally) should also display land hunger. This pattern of results would allow the investigator to reject land hunger as a possible explanation of revolts, because revolts are absent in the second set.

This is another type of paired comparison. It has the form: "even though it appears that X (land hunger) may be the cause of Y (peasant revolt) in country A, it is not, because country B has X (land hunger) but lacks Y (peasant revolt)." If all competing explanations can be rejected in this manner, Mill reasoned, then the conclusions reached by the indirect method of difference are reinforced, for true experimental design (Mill's method of difference) has been approximated. Thus, the indirect method of difference has three distinct phases: two applications of the method of agreement (the cross-tabulation of cause and effect) and a third phase involving the rejection of competing single-factor explanations through paired comparisons.

While this closer approximation of experimental design is preferable to the simple method of agreement, especially to Mill, it suffers some of the same liabilities as the method of agreement in situations of multiple causation. If land hunger and rapid commercialization both independently cause peasant revolts, there may be instances of revolt caused by rapid commercialization in the absence of land hunger and vice versa. If an investigator were to examine instances of land hunger, he or she would find agreement between land hunger and revolts. However, the second phase of the indirect method of difference would lead to the conclusion that land hunger is not the cause of revolts because rapid commercialization by itself—in the absence of land hunger—also causes revolts; thus, there are instances of the absence of land hunger associated with revolts. Parallel investigation of rapid commercialization would lead to parallel conclusions if there are revolts caused by land hunger in the absence of rapid commercialization. In the language of the statistical method, the cross-tabulation of the outcome with either causal variable would lead to independent rejection of both variables.

The reliance of the indirect method of difference on negative cases to reject competing arguments, as discussed above, is also flawed. Neither land hunger nor rapid commercialization can be rejected with instances showing an absence of revolts and a presence of one of these two factors because both independently cause revolts. The fact that neither cause can be accepted or rejected illustrates the inconclusive nature of the indirect method of difference in situations of multiple causation.

Note also that the type of paired comparison used in the third phase of the indirect method of difference is seriously incapacitated by conjunctural causation. Suppose that revolts occur when land hunger and rapid commercialization coincide and that all instances of land hunger also are instances of rapid commercialization, but not the reverse. (In essence, instances of land hunger form a subset of instances of rapid commercialization.) The investigator believes that land hunger alone causes revolts, however, and the data seem to support this conclusion. All instances of land hunger would also be instances of revolt, and all instances of the absence of land hunger would agree in showing no revolt. Further, the third phase of the indirect method of agreement would allow us to reject rapid commercialization as a cause of revolts because some instances of the absence of revolts display rapid commercialization without land hunger. In other words, the paired comparison of a positive instance (where land hunger and rapid commercialization combined to produce a revolt) with a negative instance (where rapid commercialization without land hunger failed to produce a revolt) leads to the rejection of rapid commercialization as a cause of revolts, when in fact it is the coincidence of land hunger and rapid commercialization that causes revolts. This pattern could not be observed because the investigator believed land hunger alone to be sufficient to cause a revolt. Thus, conjunctural causation seriously debilitates the type of paired comparison involved in the third phase of the indirect method of difference.

The major point of contrast between the indirect method of difference and the method of agreement is that the indirect method uses negative cases to reinforce conclusions drawn from positive cases. Generally, the indirect method is preferred to the method of agreement, but in some types of investigation the set of negative cases is ill-defined and the indirect method cannot be used. The examination of negative cases presupposes a theory allowing the investigator to identify the set of observations that embraces *possible* instances of the phenomenon of interest. Ideally, the definition of this set should not be influenced by knowledge of instances of hypothesized causes or instances of the effect.

It is often impossible in case-oriented inquiry to define such inclusive sets because an interest in specific cases or in specific categories of cases often motivates research. For example, it would be difficult to define the set that includes all negative instances of social revolution. Skocpol (1979), for example, uses nineteenth-century Germany as a negative instance of social revolution and compares this case with positive instances (France, Russia, and China). However, Germany did experience a massive upheaval in 1917–1918 that came close to being a full-blown social revolution. Thus, Germany is borderline at best as a negative instance. Because the selection of negative cases is arbitrary in the absence of strong theoretical or substantive guidelines, investigators who are interested in unusual or extreme outcomes tend to rely on the method of agreement. (For these reasons, Tilly 1984 correctly views Skocpol's approach as a "universalizing" strategy, his term for the method of agreement.)

MULTIPLE AND CONJUNCTURAL CAUSATION IN CASE-ORIENTED RESEARCH

These two methods, the method of agreement and the indirect method of difference, form the core of the case-oriented strategy. While they are both useful, especially as inductive techniques, both appear to be incapable of handling multiple or conjunctural causation, at least in the simple and relatively abstract versions presented above. If multiple conjunctural causation is in fact common, as argued in the previous chapter, why should these case-oriented techniques remain popular? What explains their continued use?

Case-oriented methods are used primarily to identify invariant relationships. They are used to pinpoint patterns of constant association, not to explain variation. Because of causal complexity, however, it is difficult to identify invariant relationships that are neither circular nor trivial. Typically, therefore, when the method of agreement or the indirect method of difference is applied in a mechanical fashion to the evidence, the investigator's initial argument is disproved. If the investigator has reason to believe that the argument has at least an element of truth to it, however, then it is not likely to be discarded. Usually, a dialogue between the investigator's ideas and the evidence develops. The initial rejection of preliminary arguments is simply the first step in this dialogue. Often such rejections constitute the anomaly to be explained and may become the primary focus of an investigation.

Several options are available to case-oriented investigators once preliminary hypotheses have been rejected. Investigators can refine their arguments and try to effect a better fit with the evidence. Suppose, for example, that the initial argument is that a certain outcome follows a coincidence of three preconditions, and the investigator finds that all instances of the outcome agree in displaying a coincidence of these three. Suppose also, however, that there are instances of the absence of the outcome which also display the same three preconditions. Rather than discard the initial formulation of the hypothesis, the investigator at this point might try to identify additional conditions relevant to the outcome that must accompany the original three. If, for example, all instances of the outcome agree in an additional precondition, and instances of an absence of the outcome displaying the original three preconditions agree in not displaying the fourth condition, then the investigator could report that the evidence supports a more elaborate argument than initially proposed. The investigator in this example successfully narrows the range of empirical conditions relevant to an outcome from a coincidence of three conditions to a coincidence of four.

Other responses to rejections of preliminary hypotheses are possible. An application of the method of agreement may show that instances of a certain outcome display no common causes. Confronted with this initial rejection, the investigator may search for differences among instances of the outcome that may have been overlooked. Perhaps the investigator originally assumed that all outcomes identified as instances of the phenomenon of interest (as instances of ethnic political mobilization, for example) were identical or at least of the same type, when in fact several different types exist. The investigator would then try to delineate these types (that is, types of ethnic mobilization) and then determine the different combinations of causes relevant to each type.

Suppose an investigator is trying to identify the causes of national revolts in Third World countries (see Walton 1984) and has collected information on the causes of all major national revolts. The method of agreement may show no common cause or set of causes. Rather than conclude that there are no invariant relationships, the investigator may suspect that there are different types of national revolts and that different sets of causes are relevant to each type. In a reanalysis of the evidence, the investigator would attempt to establish these different types by using the method of agreement to show invariant relationships within each type. The indirect method of difference would then be used to distinguish between types. Thus, multiple causation is addressed by reconceptualizing the phenomenon of interest so that types can be distinguished. Used in this manner, case-oriented methods provide a powerful basis not only for identifying causes but also for differentiating among important types and subtypes of social phenomena.

This second strategy is often used when negative cases are difficult to define. In order to use the indirect method of difference to study revolutions, it might be necessary to identify negative cases (that is, instances of an absence of revolution) because the double application of the method of agreement, which comprises the first two phases of the indirect method, requires positive and negative cases. As noted above, however, the set of nonrevolutions is virtually infinite, and it would be difficult to construct a list of nonrevolutions that would satisfy all critics. This problem exists in many comparative investigations. The set that contains all instances of the failure to form an ethnic political party is also difficult to define. It is possible to identify successful formations; delineating the class of nonformations is problematic. One solution is to identify types. The indirect method of difference can then be applied to types because instances of other types provide negative cases whenever the conditions relevant to a certain type are assessed. Tilly (1984) would describe this as an exercise in "finding variation."

Generally, unanticipated differences among positive cases can be addressed by differentiating types and assessing patterns of multiple causation, while the analysis of patterns of conjunctural causation (that is, combinations of causes) provides a basis for elaborating the crucial differences between positive and negative cases. The method of agreement and the indirect method of difference, therefore, provide rough guidelines for the conduct of comparative inquiry, especially for carrying on a dialogue with the evidence. They are not used in a rigid or mechanical manner in most case-oriented investigations.

It is important to distinguish, therefore, between formal characteristics of case-oriented methods, as formulated by Mill and others, and their application. Formally, they tend to be incapacitated by either multiple or conjunctural causation if used in a rigid manner; in practice, such apparent failures of case-oriented methods provide opportunities for the development of new theoretical and empirical distinctions and for the elaboration of historical models and types.

CASE-ORIENTED METHODS IN PRACTICE

In practice, case-oriented methods often stimulate the development of new substantive theories. The theory-generative nature of case-oriented inquiry is evident even in its most basic application—the use of the method of agreement to resolve a simple paradox. Characteristically, this paradox has the form: "objects A and B are different. Yet they both experienced outcome Y. What causally relevant similarities between A and B explain this common outcome?" The goal of this type of analysis is simply to identify common causes and thereby explain a common outcome. Only when A and B are very different is it difficult to identify common causes. The more A and B differ, the greater the apparent paradox and the more challenging the task of identifying the common underlying causal factors.

An excellent example of this type of simple paradox resolution is found in Marvin Harris's (1978) investigation of various "sociocultural puzzles." For example, Harris studied specific meat taboos in several regions of the world. From a Western point of view many of these taboos seem bizarre, and traditional explanations of these practices cite religious beliefs. Harris rejects these arguments as unscientific because a different belief system is cited in the explanation of each taboo. As a substitute for particularistic explanations, Harris is able to show that in each case the emergence of these practices resulted from ecological pressures and crises. These ecological crises, in turn, are traced to tensions between the technology of food production and human reproduction. Thus, a common outcome, religiously proscribed foods, is explained in a variety of different settings with a single overarching framework emphasizing the interplay of social and ecological constraints. In the course of showing the underlying similarities among these different settings, Harris is able to dispose of particularistic, culturalist explanations of certain food taboos.

There are three basic steps in this research strategy. First, the investigator searches for underlying similarities among members of a set displaying some common outcome (or any characteristic of interest). Second, the similarities identified are shown to be causally relevant to the phenomenon of interest. And third, on the basis of the similarities identified, the investigator formulates a general explanation. In short, it is a straightforward application of the method of agreement. It is deductive because initial theoretical notions serve as guides in the examination of causally relevant similarities and differences. (Without theoretical guides, the search for similarities and differences could go on forever.) It is inductive because the investigator determines which of the theoretically relevant similarities and differences are operative by examining empirical cases. In this phase of the investigation the researcher formulates a general explanation on the basis of identified similarities. Thus, induction culminates in concept formation and the elaboration of initial theoretical ideas.

Harris makes it look simple. But the results of applications of this strategy are rarely so neat. More typically, the process of identifying underlying similarities and differences is anything but straightforward. The problem is that the mechanical identification of similarities and differences rarely provides very much in the way of raw material for producing a satisfactory resolution of the initial paradox. Obvious similarities, which may be few in number, may be causally irrelevant to the outcome of interest or may be too general to provide a satisfactory basis for formulating an adequate explanation. Furthermore, the possibility of identifying types of a phenomenon as a way of circumventing the absence of underlying commonalities is not very attractive if there are only two or three cases. The more challenging the paradox and the more dissimilar the cases, the less the likelihood that causally relevant commonalities can be easily identified.

Michael Burawoy, for example, uses a case-oriented strategy in his study of the organization of work incentives at two points in time in a Chicago industrial establishment. In his book *Manufacturing Consent: Changes in the Labor Process Under Monopoly Capitalism* (1979) he contrasts the organization of work incentives in a single factory in the 1940s and again in the 1970s. His goal is to explain how different incentive systems produce a common outcome: worker compliance with production norms. Obvious similarities are (necessarily) few. The remuneration system used in the 1940s was oriented toward actual piece rates, and a major locus of conflict was over the rate attached to each job. In the 1970s, however, a different system prevailed, and conflict centered on base earnings and fringe benefits for different jobs and on the ease with which workers could move to the higher skilled jobs. "Whereas in 1945 bargaining between management and worker over the distribution of the rewards of labor took place on the shop floor, in 1975 such bargaining had been largely transferred out of the shop and into the conference room" (Burawoy 1979 : 50).

These two systems of worker remuneration produced the same outcome—worker conformity to production norms—on virtually identical shop floors. (Despite higher productivity, *relevant* technological changes were few.) Thus, Burawoy explains a constant (worker compliance) with a variable (different ways of producing it on the shop floor). At a mechanical level, few commonalities were identified, for the two systems of incentives were fairly different. Yet the outcome was the same, and Burawoy produces a convincing social scientific account of how the same outcome was produced in different ways.

This example indicates that identification of underlying commonalities often does not involve a simple tabulation and analysis of common characteristics. Investigators must allow for the possibility that characteristics which appear different (such as qualitatively different systems of incentives) have the same consequence. They are causally equivalent at a more abstract level—at the level of the "game" that develops on the shop floor, according to Burawoy (1979 : 48–60)—but not at a directly observable level. Thus, there may be an "illusory difference" between two objects that is actually an underlying common cause when considered at a more abstract level. Allowing for the possibility of causal equivalence of apparently dissimilar features severely complicates the identification of underlying commonalities.

Another type of paradox resolution that uses a parallel case-oriented strategy involves cases with different outcomes. Two cases may appear to be very similar and yet experience different outcomes. In this type of investigation, the goal is to identify the difference that is responsible for contradictory outcomes. Instead of studying the underlying similarities between relatively dissimilar objects, the investigator studies the causally decisive differences between relatively similar objects. The basic mechanics of this type of paradox resolution are parallel to the mechanics of the first type: the investigator uses theory to aid in the identification of relevant differences; the differences identified are then shown to be causally relevant to the outcome of interest; and on the basis of the differences identified the investigator formulates or refines a general explanation of the phenomenon of interest.

Examples of this research strategy in comparative social science abound. Investigators are very concerned with matching cases as much as possible as a way to establish experiment-like designs. For example, researchers often restrict their investigations to countries that are as similar on as many theoretically relevant variables as possible. This strategy allows researchers to exclude certain types of explanations or certain confounding variables categorically. Alford (1963), for example, studied only English-speaking democracies with single-member, simple-plurality electoral systems in his study of the effect of urbanization and industrialization on the relationship between social class and party support. It was necessary to control for electoral system by holding it constant because the interpretation of the relationship between social class and party support is different in electoral systems that use proportional representation. Traditionally, this strategy has been called the "most similar nations" design.

This strategy, while experiment-like, is not without problems of its own. The first strategy, sketched above, is confounded by illusory differences—features which appear different but are causally equivalent at a more abstract level. The second strategy is confounded by the obverse of illusory difference—"illusory commonality." The identification of causally significant differences is the key to the success of the second strategy. Yet two cases may appear to share a certain feature which the investigator might identify as a commonality (and therefore irrelevant to the explanation of differences in outcomes), when in fact these apparently common features differ dramatically in causal significance.

Illusory commonalities exist whenever two features appear similar but have different effects. For example, employment tests are used by some employers as a gating mechanism to screen out illiterate workers, regardless of the level of literacy required on the job. They are used by others to identify applicants with the greatest job-relevant skills. It would be a mistake to equate these two uses in an investigation of firms' hiring practices, even though they appear to be similar. It probably would be necessary in this investigation to contextualize the interpretation of employment testing (as a variable) by taking into account associated practices and the skill levels employers require of employees. In a low-skill context, employment testing may indicate a simple interest in excluding illiterates, who from the employer's perspective may possess other "undesirable" traits (such as minority membership). In the high-skill context, employment testing may indicate a simple interest in hiring the most qualified workers. Thus, in an investigation of hiring practices, the use of employment tests may be an illusory commonality.

Both illusory difference and its obverse, illusory commonality, interfere with the identification of underlying similarities and differences. The more general class that encompasses both illusory commonality and illusory difference is multiple conjunctural causation. What makes a certain feature, a commonality, causally relevant in one setting and not in another is the fact that its causal significance is altered by the presence of other features (that is, its effect is altered by context). Similarly, apparently different features can have the same effect depending on which other features they are associated with. Such contextualization of the causal importance of different conditions is the rule, rather than the exception, in most case-oriented studies. This is a primary justification for examining cases as wholes and for trying to decipher how different causal factors fit together. By examining differences and similarities *in context* it is possible to determine how different combinations of conditions have the same causal significance and how similar causal factors can operate in opposite directions.

Such contextualized causal arguments are necessary because the problem is to explain how relatively dissimilar cases experience the same outcome or how relatively similar cases experience different outcomes. Thus, mechanically identifiable similarities and differences may be few, and the investigation must focus on how conditions combine in different settings to produce the same or different outcomes. The identification of patterns of multiple conjunctural causation provides a basis for specifying, at a more abstract level, the underlying similarities responsible for similar outcomes and the underlying differences responsible for different outcomes.

THE LIMITS OF CASE-ORIENTED INQUIRY

One of the most valuable features of the case-oriented approach, as illustrated above, is the fact that it engenders an extensive dialogue between the investigator's ideas and the data. Each case is examined as a whole, as a total situation resulting from a combination of conditions, and cases are compared with each other as wholes. This makes it possible to address causal complexes—to examine the conjunctures in time and space that produce the important social changes and other phenomena that interest social scientists and their audiences. Furthermore, case-oriented methods require that investigators suspend assumptions about the equivalence of cases and conditions. For example, it is *not* assumed at the outset of an investigation that all the cases are drawn from roughly the same population or that the meaning of various measurements (including presence/absence variables) are the same from one case to the next. This flexibility, which is the hallmark of the case-oriented approach, enriches the dialogue between ideas and evidence.

The case-oriented approach works well when the number of relevant cases is relatively small. The comparison of two to four positive cases with the same number of negative cases is manageable. As the number of cases and the number of relevant causal conditions increase, however, it becomes more and more difficult to use a case-oriented approach. When there are only a few cases, as is the rule in many comparative historical investigations, it is not difficult to identify similarities because the researcher usually has (or tries to establish) an intimate familiarity with relevant cases. For most of mainstream social science, however, such intimacy is rare. The typical survey study, for example, has hundreds of respondents; the typical quantitative cross-national study includes scores of countries. Not only does the difficulty of identifying commonalities increase, but the commonalities themselves become more scarce. As the number of cases increases, the likelihood that any given causally relevant characteristic will be common to the entire set decreases.

In *Social Origins of Dictatorship and Democracy,* one of the best examples of the case-oriented approach, for instance, Barrington Moore (1966) analyzes only eight cases. Seven of these cases are instances of successful polity modernization. Among these seven, Moore distinguishes three types: the democratic, fascist, and communist routes to the modern world. He uses the indirect method of difference to justify his assignment of these cases to the three subtypes and, at the same time, to elaborate their important similarities and differences. These seven successful cases are contrasted with an eighth, India, an apparently unsuccessful case.

While elegant, Moore's analysis is complex. He builds an intricate web of similarities and differences that is difficult to unravel. This complexity is a direct consequence of the logic of case-oriented comparative inquiry. Cases are compared as wholes with each other. As the number of cases increases, the number of possible comparisons increases geometrically. In Moore's study, which has a modest number of cases, eight, there are twenty-eight possible comparisons. A narrative that allows this many comparisons can easily get out of hand. Only a skilled comparativist can consider all the theoretically relevant similarities and differences and keep them organized. A thorough case-oriented study of twenty cases would entail almost two hundred possible comparisons.

This expanding volume of comparisons is further enlarged if the investigator considers a large number of causal conditions. Because case-oriented comparative methods are holistic, conditions are examined in combinations. As the number of relevant causal conditions increases, the number of logically possible combinations of causal conditions increases exponentially. An investigator who considers eight different causal conditions conceived in presence/absence terms, for example, might consider a maximum of 256 different combinations of these eight conditions.

While all these different combinations certainly would not exist empirically, they are relevant to speculation about the possible impact of altered circumstances (that is, they are the raw material of thought experiments). Comparative social scientists routinely consider how the presence or absence of a certain condition in a specific case might have altered the outcome it experienced. These theoretical comparisons using empirical and hypothetical cases are similar to the holistic comparisons of empirical cases. In this sense, the number of causal conditions considered increases the number of cases to be compared because it expands the set of relevant hypothetical cases. It is not surprising, therefore, that investigators who use case-oriented methods limit their investigations to small numbers of carefully selected cases and consider specific types of causal factors (instead of all possibly relevant causes). The volume of logically possible comparisons can easily get out of control if the analysis is not restricted in this way.

These observations on the limits of case-oriented methods turn Smelser's (1976) argument about the comparative method on its head. He argues that the method of systematic comparative illustration (that is, case-oriented methods) must be used when the number of relevant cases is too small to permit the use of statistical methods (see Chapter 1). The foregoing discussion suggests that the reverse is true. Because case-oriented methods compare cases with each other and consider combinations or conjunctures of causal conditions, the potential volume of the analysis increases geometrically with the addition of a single case, and it increases exponentially with the addition of a single causal condition. Thus, it is not the number of relevant cases that limits the selection of method, as Smelser argues, but the nature of the method that limits the number of cases and the number of different causal conditions that the investigator is able to consider.

SUMMARY OF THE CASE-ORIENTED STRATEGY

Investigators who use case-oriented methods often combine causal analysis, interpretive analysis, and concept formation in the course of their studies. Several distinctive features of case-oriented methods make this possible.

First, they are designed to uncover patterns of invariance and constant association. A cross-tabulation of cause and effect is accepted as definitive only if all deviating cases are accounted for in some way. Probabilistic relationships are not accepted as demonstrations of cause. This stringent requirement forces investigators to get very close to their data and become familiar with their cases as they try to pinpoint key differences between cases. The search for invariance encourages greater specificity in causal arguments and often leads to the development of important distinctions between subtypes of social phenomena.

The second distinguishing feature follows from the first: the method is relatively insensitive to the frequency distribution of types of cases. A single case can cast doubt on a cause–effect relationship established on the basis of many observations. It does not matter how many cases are in the presence/presence and absence/absence cells of the cross-tabulation of causes and effect. If a single case exists in any of the deviating cells, the causal relationship is questioned and the investigator must account for the deviation. Thus, notions of sampling and sampling distributions are less relevant to this approach because it is not concerned with the relative distribution of cases with different patterns of causes and effects. More important than relative frequency is the *variety* of meaningful patterns of causes and effects that exist.

Third, case-oriented methods force investigators to consider their cases as whole entities. Researchers examine cases as wholes, not as collections of variables. An interest in interpreting specific cases and in pinpointing the combinations of conditions, the causal complexes, that produce specific outcomes encourages investigators to view cases as wholes. Thus, the different parts or conditions that make up a case are understood in relation to each other. They are considered together as composing a single situation. This approach contrasts sharply with how they are treated in other types of investigations. In statistical analyses of large numbers of observations, for example, relations between parts are understood only in the context of analyses of the entire population or sample. That is, relations between parts are seen as derivative of sample or population properties, not in the context of the separate wholes they form. In most statistical analyses, population or sample patterns determine how the parts of a single case are understood. (This argument is developed in greater detail in Chapter 4.)

Fourth, case-oriented methods stimulate a rich dialogue between ideas and evidence. Because these methods are flexible in their approach to the evidence—few simplifying assumptions are made—they do not restrict or constrain the examination of evidence. They do not force investigators to view causal conditions as opponents in the struggle to explain variation. Rather, they provide a basis for examining how conditions combine in different ways and in different contexts to produce different outcomes.

Thus, case-oriented studies have unique strengths and they have limitations. The distinctiveness of the case-oriented approach is magnified when contrasted with the variable-oriented approach, the focus of Chapter 4.

4

The Variable-Oriented Approach

Case-oriented methods, at least as I have described them, are classic comparative methods. They are oriented toward comprehensive examination of historically defined cases and phenomena. And they emerge clearly from one of the central goals of comparative social science—to explain and interpret the diverse experiences of societies, nations, cultures, and other significant macrosocial units. The case-oriented strategy is very much an evidence-oriented strategy. Thus, flexibility in approach to evidence is a key feature of case-oriented methods. By contrast, the variable-oriented approach is theory-centered. It is less concerned with understanding specific outcomes or categories of outcomes and more concerned with assessing the correspondence between relationships discernible across many societies or countries, on the one hand, and broad theoretically based images of macrosocial phenomena, on the other.

The popularity of the variable-oriented approach in comparative social science has been maintained over the last two and a half decades by renewed interest in macrosocial theory. The 1960s and the 1970s witnessed a renaissance of ecological and evolutionary approaches (Parsons 1977; Lenski 1966, 1974; Hawley 1981); the convergence of various strains of modernization theory into a coherent macrosocial theory (Inkeles and Smith 1974; Armer and Schnaiberg 1972; Delacroix and Ragin 1978); and an explosion of interest among North American social scientists in dependency theory (Frank 1967, 1969, 1972) and its theoretical descendant, world-systems theory (Wallerstein 1974, 1979, 1980, 1984; Ragin and Chirot 1984).

The renewed interest in macrosocial theory stimulated (and was reinforced by) the effort to import quantitative techniques from mainstream social science and to use these techniques to test the theories. Investigators reasoned, correctly, that testing broad macrosocial theories would require analytic techniques capable of digesting data on many countries. The attractiveness of these techniques was enhanced by the fact that they gave comparative social science greater legitimacy and a new affinity with mainstream social science, which in turn served to counterbalance the clear ideological positions embodied in many macrosocial theories. In many respects, variable-oriented comparative work became simply a more macrosocial version of the sociology of organizations. (See, for example, Nielsen and Hannan 1977.)

This chapter examines the logic of variable-oriented techniques in comparative social science. Most of the discussion contrasts variable-oriented methods with case-oriented methods so that the differences between the two approaches are highlighted. I begin by contrasting their goals.

THE GOALS OF VARIABLE-ORIENTED COMPARATIVE RESEARCH

Behind every research effort are general goals that extend beyond the specific goals of the study at hand. These goals are seldom stated explicitly, and they are rarely examined. The goal of most comparative social science is to produce explanations of macrosocial phenomena that are general but also show an appreciation of complexity. In other words, comparative social scientists recognize that a good social scientific explanation is relevant to a variety of cases (if for no other reason than because it uses general explanatory concepts), but at the same time they recognize that social phenomena are complex and that a general explanation is a partial explanation at best. Thus, generality and complexity often compete with each other, even in a single study. An appreciation of complexity sacrifices generality; an emphasis on generality encourages a neglect of complexity. It is difficult to have both.

In the case-oriented strategies outlined in Chapter 3, it is clear that the goal of appreciating complexity is given precedence over the goal of achieving generality. Invariant statements relevant to more narrowly defined categories of phenomena, for example, are preferred to probabilistic statements relevant to broadly defined categories. In variable-oriented strategies, by contrast, generality is given precedence over complexity. This is because investigators who use this approach are more interested in testing propositions derived from general theories than they are in unraveling the historical conditions that produce different historical outcomes. The case-oriented approach uses theory to aid historical interpretation and to guide the identification of important causal factors; the variable-oriented strategy, by contrast, usually tests hypotheses derived from theory.

ELEMENTS OF THEORY TESTING IN VARIABLE-ORIENTED RESEARCH

When a theory is tested, it is necessary for the investigator to amass a substantial quantity of relevant evidence and to apply analytic techniques that are conservative by design. Because little attempt is made to gain concrete knowledge about specific cases or specific categories of historical outcomes (beyond that necessary to code variables), investigators cast a wide net; they avoid any unnecessary restriction of scope. Typically, a variable-oriented study begins by specifying the hypothesis to be tested and then delineating the widest possible population of relevant observations. The wider this population, the better. Not only does a wide population provide a basis for a more exacting test, but it also gives the investigator the opportunity to demonstrate the breadth of an argument.

In a typical variable-oriented study, the investigator examines relationships between general features of social structures conceived as variables. The implicit model of causation central to this strategy is structural. Social units, such as nation-states, have structural features which interact in the sense that changes in some features produce changes in other features, which in turn may produce changes in others. Features of social structure are viewed as more or less permanent attributes because they are thought to be very slow in changing. Thus, relations between structural features are viewed as "permanent causes" (Mill 1843) because they concern processes involving fundamental and enduring attributes of social units. Permanent causes cannot be removed for purposes of experimentation because they are linked to constituent aspects of the unit.

In this approach, data on social units provide snapshots of instances of structural processes. Thus, structural features and their interrelations can be represented in terms of variables and intercorrelations. By studying the patterns that emerge from such snapshots of structural processes (that is, by studying correlations between variables), it is possible to derive empirical generalizations about structural processes relevant to large numbers of macrosocial units (usually nation-states). Thus, explanations in the variable-oriented strategy usually cite features of social structure.

Like the case-oriented strategy, the variable-oriented strategy has a clearly identifiable logic of analysis. In the latter, this logic centers on theory testing. First, the theory to be tested must be more or less clearly specified in terms of variables and relations. Second, competing explanations of the phenomenon of interest (which typically is a social structural variable) also must be formulated in terms of variables. Competing explanations play an important part in the variable-oriented strategy because tests of preferred theories must be conservative by design; the preferred theory is tested against alternatives. Third, it is necessary to devise appropriate measures of the variables specified in the various arguments, and the investigator must ascertain the reliability and validity of these measures. Finally, statistical analyses of the relationships between these measures, based on data from a systematically selected set of observations, are used to test the theory against alternative explanations. Statistical analyses of correlations between variables (both cross-sectional and longitudinal) provide a basis for empirical generalizations about structural processes specified in theories. Correlational analysis provides explicit operationalization of principles of structural causation.

An important feature of statistical analysis relevant to the variable-oriented strategy is the central (but often implicit) goal of parsimony. An explanation citing only a few variables is preferred to one citing many—as long as the more parsimonious explanation is a plausible specification of the phenomenon of interest and as long as the variables added by the more elaborate explanation do not significantly increase the proportion of explained variation in the dependent variable. (See Lieberson 1985 for a critique of methods that use proportion of explained variation as a fundamental criterion for evaluating models.) Thus, statistical analysis should keep the number of explanatory variables to a minimum. Explanations based on statistical analysis, therefore, focus on dominant patterns that emerge from a broad view of a phenomenon in a variety of settings. The confounding effects of local, particularistic factors are often conceived as error (see Ragin and Zaret 1983). This way of conceiving error is consistent with the overall strategy of achieving generality at the expense of comprehending or appreciating complexity.

APPLICATION OF QUANTITATIVE TECHNIQUES TO CROSS-NATIONAL DATA

The emphasis of the variable-oriented strategy on general features of social structure, conceived as variables, and on testing theory, as opposed to using theory to interpret cases historically, has allowed importation of quantitative methods, especially multiple regression techniques, from mainstream social science. These are powerful techniques. They allow investigators to make broad statements about cross-societal patterns on the basis of analyses of relatively small data sets. (The typical quantitative cross-national data set contains fewer than eighty cases and ten variables—a tiny data set by the standards of mainstream social science.) Investigators are able to formulate broad generalizations about such important issues as international inequality on the basis of analyses of such data.

From the perspective of mainstream social science, the importation of multivariate statistical techniques has benefited comparative social science in a number of ways. First, it has allowed comparative social scientists to study more than a handful of cases at a time. The application of case-oriented methods to a large number of cases is difficult because case-oriented methods encourage investigators to compare each case with every other case and with relevant hypothetical cases. This strategy greatly expands the volume of the analysis (see Chapter 3). Furthermore, case-oriented methods require investigators to be very familiar with their cases as separate entities; the variable-oriented strategy does not demand a comparable level of familiarity. (Of course, such familiarity certainly enhances the quality of variable-oriented research.)

Second, it has spurred a new interest in reliable quantitative cross-national data. This interest is beneficial because quantification allows more rigorous tests of theory to be performed. Quantification of features of social structure provides a basis for testing broad theories about relations between structural properties.

Third, it has allowed investigators to consider alternative explanations more carefully when testing a theory. Case-oriented methods are sometimes criticized for restricting the consideration of alternative explanations. This is especially likely if the primary goal of an investigation is interpretive (Skocpol and Somers 1980). By contrast, the consideration of alternative explanations is an important part of all variable-oriented investigations because the rejection of alternative explanations plays an essential role in demonstrating the preferred explanation.

Fourth, it has socialized comparative social science. No longer is knowledge of countries the special province of area specialists. Cross-national data banks, especially those specializing in aggregate data, are easily accessible to all investigators. Thus, it is a simple matter to evaluate the findings of other researchers. The results of case-oriented studies, by contrast, tend to be very personal.

Fifth, it has made comparative social science more cautious in formulating empirical generalizations. The quantitative techniques that have been imported are conservative by design; this characteristic is inherent in the statistical models that have been used. Typically, the independent variables used are strongly correlated, which makes it difficult to assign cause unambiguously and also decreases the likelihood that any single variable will have a significant effect. Furthermore, significance tests, which are central to this approach, favor rejecting rather than accepting hypothesized relationships.

Sixth, it has counteracted the tendency among some comparativists to favor particularistic explanations when faced with many deviating cases. There is no requirement in statistical analysis that investigators must account for all cases. Statistical methods assume that causal relationships are at best probabilistic, and outliers are expected.

And, finally, it has allowed investigators to use techniques of statistical control. This last point is the most important and requires considerable elaboration.

PRINCIPLES OF STATISTICAL CONTROL IN CROSS-NATIONAL RESEARCH

A key feature of variable-oriented methods is their emphasis on statistical control. Statistical control is very different from experimental control, even though important differences between the two have become blurred (Lieberson 1985). Most social scientists tend to equate the two as devices that allow investigators to "hold" confounding factors "constant" while examining the effect of one variable on another. There are several features of statistical control, however, which distinguish it from experimental control and compromise its use in comparative social science.

In the typical multivariate statistical analysis, the investigator attempts to assess the effect of an independent variable on a dependent variable net of the effects of control variables (that is, other independent variables). The basic idea is that even though the independent and control variables cannot be manipulated, as they are in an experiment, it is possible to subtract the effects of control variables on the dependent variable when estimating the effect of a specific causal variable.

In most statistical analyses, the effect of a control variable is its average effect on the dependent variable, across all cases, net of the effects of other variables. The subtraction of effects central to statistical control is a purely mechanical operation predicated on simplifying assumptions. It is assumed in multiple regression, for example, that a variable's effect is the same in each case—that a one-unit change in an independent variable has the same effect on the dependent variable regardless of context, that is, regardless of the values of the other independent variables. This makes it possible to estimate and then remove a variable's effect by simple subtraction. The result is a dependent variable whose values have been "corrected" for the effects of one or more independent variables.

The results of Bornschier and others (1978), for example, show that underdeveloped countries with higher levels of domestic investment grow faster. Specifically, for every percentage point increase in capital formation (computed as a percentage of GNP) underdeveloped countries increase their economic growth rates by about three-hundredths of a percentage point. Armed with this knowledge, it is possible to correct economic growth rates for the effects of domestic investment. To remove the effect of domestic investment, it is necessary simply to subtract the quantity—capital formation as a percentage of GNP multiplied by 0.03—from each country's economic growth rate. The resulting values show economic growth rates corrected for the effect of domestic investment.

Note that the comparisons that are performed in statistical analyses such as the one described here involve contrasts between cases' scores on the relevant variables with average or mean scores. This makes it possible to compute simple and partial correlations and to calculate the relevant effects. No attempt is made to compare cases directly to each other. Only broad patterns of covariation are assessed. When quantitatively oriented researchers examine individual cases, it is usually by plotting the residuals from a multivariate regression analysis and then devoting special attention to the cases that deviate strongly from predicted patterns. Thus, the particularity of a case is defined relative to a general pattern specified through multivariate analysis.

Consider a more elaborate example of variable-oriented research. An investigator might wish to test the argument that the presence of democratic institutions gives polities greater longevity. To test the effect of the presence of democratic institutions on years of polity existence (measured as number of years without a major regime change; see Gurr 1974), it would be necessary to remove the effect of confounding variables in order to have a proper assessment of the effect of democratic institutions. For example, wealth of the nation-state might correlate with the presence of democratic institutions and also increase polity longevity. The effect of wealth, therefore, should be removed when estimating the effect of democratic institutions. Another factor which might increase polity longevity and correlate with the presence of democratic institutions is scope of state action. Scope of state action refers to the government's degree of involvement in the lives of its subjects. Because many polities with democratic institutions have states that are broad in scope, and scope is a plausible cause of longevity, the effect of scope also should be removed. And other causes of polity longevity, including such factors as period of initial polity formation, that might be confounded with the presence of democratic institutions could be identified. Measures of all such factors should be included in the statistical analysis of polity longevity and should be controlled statistically when the assessment of the effect of democratic institutions is made.

Note that to estimate these effects it is not necessary to have data on all logically possible combinations of values of the independent variables. (This is impossible, of course, if the measures are continuous.) This is one of the major attractions of statistical control. With these techniques it is possible to infer a variable's effect in all contexts simply by assessing its effect in existing settings. Thus, broad claims can be made on the basis of data that are very incomplete relative to the experimental design standard.

The mechanics of statistical control are relatively straightforward. Effect parameters for independent variables are calculated so that the correlation of the dependent variable with an additive (or, in a few studies, logarithmic) combination of the independent variables is maximized. The effect parameters (say, standardized regression coefficients) indicate the relative importance of the different independent variables. The larger the effect parameter, the more important the variable. If the control variables are the most important variables in the additive combination of independent variables, then the variable of theoretical interest (in this example, presence of democratic institutions) may have no significant effect. If this occurs, the investigator may conclude that it is not an important cause of variation in the phenomenon of interest.

A statistical analysis of polity longevity might show that the presence of democratic institutions—on the average, controlling for wealth of the nation-state, the scope of its government, and its date of origin—increases polity longevity by five years. The investigator would conclude that democracy contributes moderately to longevity. The relative impact of the three control variables on the effect of democratic institutions can be assessed by comparing the estimated effect of the variable of theoretical interest in the absence of the controls. For example, if an analysis excluding control variables were to show that the presence of democratic institutions increases polity longevity by twenty-five years, the investigator might argue that much of the apparent effect of democratic institutions on longevity is actually due to variables it is confounded with, such as the wealth of nations.

This example illustrates the broad sweep afforded by a multivariate statistical approach. By making the appropriate simplifying assumptions about unit changes and additivity, investigators can use methods that digest data on many countries and culminate in general statements of empirical regularity.

STATISTICAL VERSUS EXPERIMENTAL CONTROL

How does multivariate statistical analysis stack up against the ideal social scientific comparison embodied in logic of experimental design (see Chapters 1 and 2)? While multivariate techniques of statistical control are rigorous, statistical control is qualitatively different from experimental control and implies a substantially different type of comparison. Furthermore, the assumptions of this type of comparison may be inconsistent with some of the distinctive goals of comparative social science.

First, and obviously, the dependent variable is not examined under all possible combinations of values of the independent variables, as is possible in experimental investigations. Nonexperimental data rarely exhaust the logically possible combinations of values. (This is clearly the case when continuous, interval-scale measures are used because no technique could exhaust logically possible combinations.) Even if the interval-scale independent variables in this example were categorized into four levels of wealth, four levels of government scope, four periods of polity origin, and presence/absence of democratic institutions (a crude and perhaps unwarranted simplification), the four-way cross-tabulation of the independent variables would culminate in an abundance of empty cells. For example, almost all polities of recent origin are medium to very high in government scope and medium to low in wealth. Of course, these empty cells do not pose a grave problem if the additive linear model is an appropriate representation of the phenomenon of interest (polity longevity). Techniques of statistical control are always available to the investigator willing to make the necessary simplifying assumptions. However, it is important to consider the discontinuity between this type of model and the model implicit in experimental design, where all combinations of values on the independent variables are examined. (Note that this discussion does not address an additional problem in the analysis of nonexperimental social data—selectivity; see Lieberson 1985.)

Second, the number of cases in most of the nonempty cells is likely to be small. With democratic institutions treated as a simple presence/absence dichotomy and the other variables divided into four categories, the total number of combinations of values on the independent variables is 128, while the total number of relevant polities would probably be around 300. (Most countries have experienced a series of major regime changes and therefore have had more than one polity; see Gurr 1974.) Thus, even the nonempty cells would probably have only a few observations each, further complicating the statistical assessment of longevity. Again, this problem is circumvented by using interval-scale variables and by assuming that the relation has a specific functional form that can be estimated additively and linearly. These simplifying assumptions are not always warranted, however, despite their convenience.

Third, because the analysis is additive (and probably necessarily so, given the shortage of degrees of freedom), it assumes that the meaning of scores on the independent variables is the same across all cases regardless of the values of other independent variables. For example, the contribution of democratic institutions to political longevity in this hypothetical analysis is assumed to be the same regardless of whether government scope is broad or narrow, regardless of whether it is a newer polity or polity originating at an earlier point in time, and regardless of whether the polity is situated in a rich or a poor nation-state. One could easily hypothesize that democratic institutions would not contribute to the longevity of more recently formed polities or to the longevity of polities in poor countries. This assumption of equivalent effects applies as well to other independent variables. For example, the contribution of wealth to polity longevity is assumed to be the same regardless of whether the scope of the government's action is broad or narrow. In short, statistical control in additive models (which must be used when the number of cases is modest) must assume that context, as conceived here, is not relevant. In other words, this type of statistical control assumes that a certain effect exists independent of context, that is, independent of the values of the other causal variables in each case.

A fourth inconsistency between multivariate statistical control and the experimental design standard that is relevant to comparative social science concerns the problem of specifying relevant observations. The hypothetical analysis presented above addresses polity longevity and presumably is relevant to all polities. The normal practice would be to collect available data on all polities and treat this data set as a close approximation to the population of relevant observations. The statistical analysis, in effect, would provide a basis for estimating population parameters relevant to the prediction of polity longevity.

But is an estimate of population parameters, per se, desirable? The estimation of such parameters is powerfully influenced by the relative frequency of different types of cases. Suppose, for example, that the data set contains a large number of (1) poor, recent, democratic polities with governments of wide scope and (2) rich, democratic polities in countries from a much earlier period of initial formation, with governments of narrower scope, and that both of these polity types are relatively short-lived. (Remember that most countries have experienced a series of polities.) The estimate of the effect of democratic institutions on polity longevity would be negative. This finding would be obtained regardless of other patterns in the data. (Other patterns might be revealed, of course, if the investigator were to examine residuals.) Paired comparisons, such as those used in case-oriented investigations, of the remaining cases might show, however, that the presence of democratic institutions consistently increases longevity in a variety of settings. The much greater relative frequency of the first two types mentioned above would statistically outweigh the positive contributions of democratic institutions in other types of settings.

To the extent that comparative researchers are more interested in the effect of a variable in different settings or in different types of cases—and less interested in its average, net effect in a population of observations—techniques of statistical control produce findings that are of unknown value. Use of these techniques, therefore, must be predicated on an interest in population parameters—the average effect of a cause in a theoretically defined set of observations.

Finally, the model of causation implicit in additive multivariate statistical techniques contradicts notions of multiple conjunctural causation. As described in previous chapters, multiple conjunctural causation involves multiple intersections of causal conditions. In multivariate statistical models, by contrast, the model of causation, while crudely multiple, is typically additive, not conjunctural. In an additive multivariate model, the goal is to estimate the separate contribution of each cause. Different causes increase or decrease the probability or level of a certain outcome independently of one another.

An investigator might determine, for example, that the presence of X_1 increases the probability of Y by 10 percent, while the presence of X_2 increases the probability of Y by 15 percent, while X_3 and X_4 have no effect on the probability of Y. Together X_1 and X_2 might increase the probability of Y by 25 percent. This goal of estimating each cause's independent contribution to the probability of Y is inconsistent with the goal of determining the different combinations of conditions that cause Y. An examination of combinations might show, for example, that X_1 causes Y only when it coincides with both X_3 and X_4, and that X_2 causes Y only when it coincides with an absence of X_4, and that these two patterns are invariant. Estimation of the independent contribution of different causes to the probability of an outcome does not address concerns for multiple conjunctural causation.

To summarize: statistical control is very different from experimental control. The consequences of these differences are most apparent in comparative research, where instances of causal complexity abound. While statistical control allows investigators to make broad statements with relatively little data, these broad statements are possible only because very powerful simplifying assumptions have been made. Furthermore, the character of these broad statements is shaped directly by the character of the method. That is, these methods culminate in probabilistic statements about a variable's average, net effect in a wide variety (typically a population or sample) of settings.

RESPONSES TO CRITICISMS OF STATISTICAL CONTROL

From the perspective of mainstream social science the first two problems presented above plague all nonexperimental investigations and cannot be addressed within a statistical framework. Multivariate techniques were developed in the social sciences precisely because social phenomena are difficult to study experimentally, and naturally occurring data that approximate data resulting from experimental designs are extremely rare. Techniques of statistical control, therefore, should not be criticized because the data sets analyzed by social scientists are deficient. In other words, techniques of statistical control should not be criticized for their failure to address problems they were designed to circumvent.

The remaining deficiencies of multivariate statistical control outlined above can be remedied through more sophisticated techniques. However, the data used by comparativists often are not strong enough to permit these remedies. For example, the third problem listed above concerns the likelihood that a certain independent variable will have different effects on the outcome variable depending on the values of other independent variables. In short, the effect of a variable (say, the effect of democratic institutions on polity longevity) may depend on context (whether the country is rich or poor, whether its government is active in many spheres or few, and so on). Most experts in multivariate techniques would suggest that researchers who suspect such patterns of contextuality test for them by using interaction models. These models allow investigators to assess the different effects of one variable on another within categories of a third variable. In other words, experts would argue that investigators should use statistical models that do not assume additivity.

Interaction models also can be used to address the fifth concern listed above: the problem of multiple conjunctural causation. Essentially, an interaction model allows a direct statistical test of the argument that the effect of a variable varies by context (that is, its effect depends on the values of other independent variables). The idea of conjunctural causation asserts simply that some causes are effective only in the presence of others. Causal conjunctures can be represented in statistical analyses as interaction terms and tested against additive formulations.

However, statistical tests for interaction work well only when all empirically plausible interactions are known in advance (that is, can be hypothesized), when there is a relatively small number of such interactions, when hypothesized interactions are not excessively collinear with each other, when a simple additive model is an empirically plausible representation of other causes of the phenomenon of interest, and when the number of cases is large enough to allow the investigator to assess the strength of the interaction effect relative to linear approximations.

Most data used by comparative social scientists, even data used by comparativists devoted to the use of techniques of statistical control, do not meet these requirements. For example, the use of interaction models to examine multiple conjunctural causation is difficult because of an insufficiency of cases and because the interaction terms used to assess the intersection of different causal conditions usually are highly collinear with each other. An examination of different combinations of six different causal conditions, for example, would require an equation with sixty-four terms, many of which would be highly collinear because of their common component terms. Even if such an equation could be estimated, it would be very difficult to decipher because the coefficients could be interpreted only in groups. The data used in most comparative investigations are simply not strong enough to support tests for complex patterns of interaction. (Of course, roughly parallel problems exist in case-oriented research, where there is a corresponding limited variety of cases; see Chapter 3. Chapters 7 and 8 suggest a tentative solution to this problem.)

The fourth problem with statistical control mentioned above concerns the distorting effect that the relative frequency of different types of cases has on the estimation of population parameters. This problem can also be addressed with more sophisticated statistical techniques. One simple way to address this issue is to estimate different models for different subpopulations and test the statistical significance of the differences obtained. In an analysis of polity longevity, for example, an investigator might hypothesize that polities created before World War II are qualitatively different from polities created after World War II and that, accordingly, different models of polity longevity should be estimated for the two subpopulations. The population of polities also could be divided in other ways, depending on which subpopulation differences concern the investigator. (In essence, this is a type of interaction model.)

Again, however, the fact that most quantitative cross-national studies have relatively few cases (around fifty to one hundred) discourages investigators from splitting their samples. The greater the specificity of an argument, the fewer the number of cases available for statistical analysis. These limitations discourage the kind of specificity associated with sample splitting. Furthermore, some methodologists argue that it is necessary for the investigator to specify subpopulations in advance of data analysis. Subpopulation differences do surface in the course of variable-oriented analyses as they do in case-oriented studies (where the search for invariance forces investigators to differentiate types), but there are strong pressures on the variable-oriented researcher to keep sample splitting to a minimum.

Thus, while it is possible to answer the criticisms of statistical control and to point to more sophisticated techniques, investigators typically cannot take advantage of these techniques. Investigators are not limited to simple, linear additive models; in practice, however, they usually stick fairly close to such formulations. If any tests for interaction or for population differences are performed, they are very simple in nature. (See, for example, Chirot and Ragin 1975; Paige 1975; Delacroix and Ragin 1978.) This is because most data sets used by comparativists place serious constraints on statistical sophistication.

CONCLUSION: THE DIALOGUE OF IDEAS AND EVIDENCE IN VARIABLE-ORIENTED RESEARCH

Techniques of statistical control, and multivariate analysis in general, exercise a powerful influence on the dialogue of ideas and evidence in quantitative cross-national research. The basic building blocks of this strategy are variables and their intercorrelation. Discussions of specification issues, therefore, dominate the dialogue of ideas and evidence. Is the theory to be tested properly operationalized? Have all the appropriate control variables and competing theories been specified? Is the population of relevant observations accurately delineated? Is the sample appropriate? Has there been any unwarranted restriction of scope? Does an adequate basis for generalization exist? Are the functional forms correct? Does a plot of the residuals show that anything major has been missed? In short, the methodological issues that dominate variable-oriented investigations converge with those of mainstream social science.

How do investigators who use the variable-oriented strategy respond to rejections of initial hypotheses? In case-oriented studies, investigators typically propose more intricate conjunctural arguments or they attempt to differentiate subtypes of the phenomenon of interest and elaborate subtype-specific causal arguments. In variable-oriented studies, the response usually is quite different. Formally at least, a rejection is a rejection, and the logic of hypothesis testing central to the variable-oriented approach dictates "failure to reject" the null hypothesis. In practice, however, investigators usually try different specifications of the same argument in the hope that one will support the favored theory. Usually, this process involves adding or subtracting control variables, or reconceptualizing the key concepts of the theoretical model that is being tested, or devising new measures, or redefining control variables as theoretical variables. In short, the dialogue usually stays focused on variables and their interrelations.

Sometimes investigators using the variable-oriented strategy follow the lead of case-oriented investigators and differentiate subtypes or construct conjunctural arguments. But the pressure to use these strategies is less acute because there is no expectation that the research will culminate with an identification of invariant relationships. In any event, these case-oriented techniques sacrifice precious degrees of freedom and weaken the variable-oriented approach. Differentiating subtypes entails sample splitting and a consequent reduction of the total degrees of freedom. Likewise, constructing elaborate interaction models to test conjunctural arguments exacts a severe toll on degrees of freedom and creates an indecipherable mass of multi-collinearity. The number of terms in an equation increases exponentially as the complexity of the interaction terms to be tested increases.

At this point, the limitations of the variable-oriented strategy converge morphologically with the limitations of the case-oriented strategy in a peculiar manner. Recall that the case-oriented strategy, because it is holistic, becomes more difficult to use as the number of cases increases. The volume of comparison explodes as the number of empirical and hypothetical cases is expanded. The method simply becomes unwieldy. A morphologically parallel problem incapacitates the variable-oriented strategy. As the complexity of the causal argument to be tested increases, intractable methodological problems are introduced. Complex conjunctural arguments cannot be tested, nor can subtypes be differentiated, in the absence of sufficient cases to permit statistical manipulation. The assumptions of statistical models become more strained in the face of intricate causal arguments, given a restricted sample size. In some investigations the number of parameters to be estimated can easily exceed the number of cases, and the possibility of estimating parameters is closed off.

This chapter and the preceding chapter have presented the two main strategies in their pure, and exaggerated, forms. In Chapter 5, I discuss strategies which combine the two main approaches. Combined strategies have emerged in part because of the limitations inherent in these two approaches.

5

Combined Versus Synthetic
Comparative Strategies

Chapters 3 and 4 present two general strategies of comparative research and discuss their strengths and weaknesses. The two strategies are surprisingly complementary. The case-oriented strategy is best suited for identifying invariant patterns common to relatively small sets of cases; the variable-oriented strategy is best suited for assessing probabilistic relationships between features of social structures, conceived as variables, over the widest possible population of observations. The main weakness of the case-oriented strategy is its tendency toward particularizing (often while pretending to great generality—for example, a theory of ethnic political mobilization based on one case); the main weakness of the variable-oriented strategy is its tendency toward abstract, and sometimes vacuous, generalizations. The case-oriented strategy is incapacitated by a large number of cases; the variable-oriented strategy is incapacitated by complex, conjunctural causal arguments requiring the estimation of the effects of a large number of interaction terms or the division of a sample into many separate subsamples.

In this chapter I discuss combined strategies and the differences between combined strategies and the synthetic strategy proposed in the remainder of this work. An investigation that uses a combined strategy simply applies both major strategies to a specific problem. A synthetic strategy, by contrast, should integrate several features of case-oriented and variable-oriented approaches.

THE VALUE OF COMBINED AND SYNTHETIC STRATEGIES

Among social scientists who claim to be comparativists, the strongest contrast is between those who identify themselves as area specialists and those who regard themselves as generalists interested in dimensions of cross-national variation. These are two ends of a single continuum along which a variety of types of research can be arrayed. In between the two extremes are scholars who use case-oriented comparative methods, ranging from those who compare two or three cases to those who conduct comparative studies of many countries. At present this continuum is confounded, imperfectly, with the qualitative/quantitative continuum. Generalists tend to be quantitatively oriented; area specialists tend to be qualitatively oriented.

The most common combined research strategy is one that somehow violates this order—a case study that includes quantitative analyses, for example. There are very good reasons why this unidimensional ordering of strategies of comparative social science should be violated. Case studies tend to be very sensitive to human agency and to social processes in general. These studies tend see outcomes in terms of specific actions at specific historical junctures. Structural explanations do not fare well in case studies precisely because many important structural variables may change very slowly, if at all, within a single case. Thus, it is difficult to observe variation in these variables. This explains, in part, the well-known bias of traditional political histories toward explanations citing the actions of elites, political leaders, and so forth.

Wide-ranging cross-national studies, by contrast, are biased in favor of structural explanations. Not only is human agency obscured in studies of many cases, but the methods themselves tend to disaggregate cases into variables, distributions, and correlations. There is little room left for historical process—that is, for the active construction by humans of their history. Thus, the two ends of the methodological continuum have clear theoretical biases.

A study that combines strategies (for example, quantitative cross-national analysis with case studies) provides a methodological foundation for resisting these seemingly inherent theoretical and metatheoretical biases. Ideally, a combined strategy should allow the investigator to consider both structural factors and factors reflecting historical processes and human agency. In short, one strategy should check the biases of the other. (Of course, using combined strategies also raises the possibility that the results of the two approaches may be irreconcilable.)

A synthetic, as opposed to combined, strategy should yield similar fruit, perhaps with greater certainty. The comparative strategy presented in later chapters does not completely *synthesize* variable-oriented and case-oriented methods; instead it selectively unites certain features of the two. In common with the variable-oriented strategy, it allows examination of large numbers of cases. In common with the case-oriented strategy, it allows assessment of complex patterns of multiple and conjunctural causation. This merger offers the possibility of a middle road between emphasizing relationships among variables and structural explanations, on the one hand, and emphasizing the chronological particularities of cases and human agency, on the other.

In the next section I examine three examples of combined strategies. These strategies use case-oriented and variable-oriented approaches without trying to merge them into a single approach. These combined strategies are discussed so that they can be contrasted with the broadly comparative strategy I present in subsequent chapters. I conclude this chapter by discussing ideal features of such a strategy.

THREE COMBINED STRATEGIES

The differences between case-oriented and variable-oriented strategies are profound and not easily reconciled. Nevertheless, various combined strategies have emerged in recent years which use both general strategies. While these combined strategies overcome some of the liabilities of the two general strategies, they are not distinct strategies but are, instead, amalgamations. Quantitative cross-sectional and time-series analyses, for example, are sometimes used to buttress primarily interpretive, case-oriented investigations (see, for example, Shorter and Tilly 1974; Hechter 1975; Ragin 1979; Hage 1975), and interpretive case studies are sometimes used to support the findings of quantitative cross-national investigations (see, for example, Paige 1975 and Stephens 1979). These combined strategies are often very fruitful, but they are not distinct from the two main strategies; they simply use both. To illustrate, I discuss Shorter and Tilly's *Strikes in France, 1830–1968*, Paige's *Agrarian Revolution: Social Movements and Export Agriculture in the Underdeveloped World*, and Stephens's *The Transition from Capitalism to Socialism*.

STRIKES IN FRANCE. Two main goals are apparent in Shorter and Tilly's work: to test general arguments about the causes of collective action, especially strikes, and to chart the history and course of strikes in a specific country, France. The first goal calls for a variable-oriented strategy because the objective is to test competing theories. The second goal calls for a case-oriented strategy because the objective is to understand a specific case. Shorter and Tilly's approach is to apply statistical methods to data on a single case as a way to test theory. Theories of strikes are formally tested with cross-sectional analyses of department data and time-series analyses of annual data; the results of these analyses are used to bolster the historical analysis of strikes in France. Shorter and Tilly also compare the changing "shape" of French strikes with those of other advanced countries to determine the extent to which France's experience is reflected in other cases. These comparisons provide a basis for verifying and refining the interpretation of strikes in France.

Theory testing is an important aspect of Shorter and Tilly's work. They first contrast "breakdown," "deprivation," and "interests" arguments on the causes of collective action. These general perspectives are used to select important cross-sectional and longitudinal variables and to construct general, testable models. In this approach, different independent variables are identified with different theories, and all the independent variables are thrown together in a contest to explain variation in the dependent variable: strikes. If one theory's variables prevail in the struggle to explain cross-sectional and longitudinal variation in the dependent variable, then that theory is not rejected, whereas the others are. In Shorter and Tilly's work, the variables identified with "interests" (mostly Marxist) arguments dominate.

Of course, there is a clear difference between using countries as observational units, as in standard applications of the variable-oriented approach (see Chapter 4), and using subnational units such as French departments. (Lieberson 1985 criticizes this practice.) When they showed the relation between urbanization and strikes at the department level, for example, Shorter and Tilly did not assume that the different departments were integrated social wholes. Still, the notion of causation implied in such analyses is structural—variation in one attribute of departments explains variation in other attributes. Thus, the underlying logic of the procedure is the same. In fact, when subnational units such as departments within a single country are used, the assumption of causal homogeneity is more easily met.

Time-series analysis, by contrast, is a comparison of a case with itself at several points in time. (Chase-Dunn and others 1982 discuss a variety of time-series applications in comparative social science.) From a general comparative perspective, this is not a very promising strategy because many of the variables that might be important to broad generalization do not vary sufficiently within a single case, even over very long periods. Rokkan (1970), for example, argues that a key factor in explaining variation in polity formation in Western Europe was the formation of national churches in some countries. This kind of variation is very difficult to study within a single case. Time-series analysis does, however, offer an advantage: it is easier to link this type of analysis to actual historical sequences and to specific longitudinal processes. Occasionally, time-series analysis can be linked to a specific historical process (say, a major transformation) or to a series of comparable historical outcomes. This possibility makes comparisons of time-series analyses across several cases, a strategy advocated by Hage (1975), an attractive alternative. (See also Chase-Dunn and others 1982.)

Shorter and Tilly's statistical analyses provide reinforcement for their loosely Marxist discussion of the history of strikes in France. Their interpretation is Marxist because they use his arguments as guides in the selection of important historical evidence. For example, Marx argues that industrialization shapes collective action by altering the conditions of solidarity and organization and by creating new, enduring grievances. In their discussion of the history of strikes in France, Shorter and Tilly, following these guidelines, examine France's industrial transformation and urbanization and present historical evidence supporting the idea that these changes influenced worker organization and action. In this fashion Marx's arguments are used in much the same way that an investigator interested in organizations might use Weber's specification of the ideal-typic bureaucracy (see Ragin and Zaret 1983) to analyze features of a specific bureaucracy. Marx's arguments, of course, do not straitjacket their selection of evidence—his arguments are simply too general to be used rigidly. However, the success of the independent variables identified with Marx in the statistical analyses justifies the use of Marxist concepts to guide the selection of evidence for more detailed historical analysis.

In Shorter and Tilly's work, therefore, historical and quantitative analyses are mutually supportive. The quantitative analyses serve as a bedrock for the use of basic Marxist concepts to guide historical analysis. The historical discussions, in turn, breathe life into the quantitative analyses, giving them purpose.

Despite the use of quantitative techniques geared for broad generalizations, the work remains very much a case study. It is a Marxist interpretation of strikes in France that is buttressed with elaborate statistical analyses; little attempt is made to generalize about strikes in advanced industrial countries (and the work of other scholars indicates that their arguments cannot be generalized). This view of Shorter and Tilly's work as a case study is supported by evidence they present. The chapter that contrasts France with other advanced countries illustrates the diversity of strike patterns across Western Europe and North America. This diversity was not addressed directly. Rather, it serves primarily to demonstrate that the changing shape of strikes in France conforms best to Shorter and Tilly's predominantly political model of strikes. Other countries conform to the French pattern in varying degrees; some not at all. Thus, Shorter and Tilly's work can best be understood as a high-powered case study. Their combined strategy uses variable-oriented techniques to test theory and enhance their case study.

Although *Strikes in France* is a case study, it has much more the flavor of a variable-oriented than a case-oriented analysis. Most historical, single-country analyses fit squarely within the domain of case-oriented studies because they are predicated on the idea that the interpretation of a specific case as a meaningful chronology is valuable. This goal is clearly secondary in *Strikes in France*, for the study is theory-centered. Indeed, there is very little sense of chronology in *Strikes in France*. While one of their objectives is to understand strikes within the context of the forging of the modern French state, the origins and character of the modern French state are not addressed—at least not in this work, though Tilly (1975, 1986) discusses this issue more directly. The modern French state is not seen as a historical outcome to be explained. Rather, Shorter and Tilly are satisfied to reject modernization and other theories and support Marxist theories of strikes. In their perspective, collective action by workers is conceived as a structural variable of considerable importance in all industrial countries (see especially their concluding remarks), and it remains their major focus. The forging of the modern French state is a larger process that impinges on and is confounded with the course of workers' collective actions and is not addressed as a historical outcome.

AGRARIAN REVOLUTION.   Paige, too, uses a combined strategy. In the first part of his work he uses a pure variable-oriented approach. Specifically, he tests a theory of agrarian unrest with data from 70 developing countries, embracing 135 agricultural export sectors. (Paige uses agricultural export sectors as an observational unit in his quantitative analyses.) The goal of these analyses is to test the idea that different ways of organizing agriculture—which to a considerable degree are specific to different types of crops—produce different, characteristic forms of agrarian unrest. In the second part of Paige's work he illustrates his theory with case studies of four export sectors in three countries, each representative of one of the major types.

Paige's theory of agrarian revolution focuses on income sources of cultivators, those who actually work the land, and income sources of noncultivators, those who form the agrarian elite or in some way dominate cultivators. These distinctions and their cross-tabulation provide a basis for specifying five types of agricultural organizations (sharecropping, migratory labor estates, commercial haciendas, plantations, and smallholding systems) and five characteristic types of agrarian unrest (revolutionary socialist, revolutionary nationalist, agrarian, labor, and commodity movements). Statistical analyses of the relationships between the frequency of different types of unrest and the presence of the different types of agricultural organization support his contention that each way of organizing agriculture has a characteristic form of unrest. This finding supports, in turn, his emphasis on the sources of income of cultivators and noncultivators as the key to understanding agrarian conflict.

This broad scope is made possible by the variable-oriented approach. By conceptualizing agricultural organization as a nominal-scale variable based on sources of cultivator and noncultivator income and by differentiating types of agrarian unrest and measuring the worldwide distribution of each type, Paige is able to construct and test a truly global model.

Although its scope was breathtaking, Paige was persuaded that this variable-oriented analysis by itself was not enough. There are those who might argue, for example, that he biased the test of his theory toward success in the way he constructed his variables. His delineation of types of agricultural organizations, for example, is based on sources of income. Do cultivators derive income from land *or* wages; do noncultivators derive income from land *or* capital? But it is entirely possible for both cultivators and noncultivators to derive income from a variety of sources and in varying amounts. Furthermore, the importance of an income source could fluctuate over time, depending on surrounding circumstances such as world market conditions or the relations between cultivators or noncultivators and the state. These circumstances themselves could influence the type and intensity of agrarian unrest. In short, while impressive, the statistical analysis by itself leaves many questions unanswered.

Paige's solution is to provide case studies which illustrate the theory. Specifically, he examines the relationship between agricultural organization and agrarian unrest in three countries: Peru, Angola, and Viet Nam. Peru provides examples of the commercial hacienda and the plantation; Angola, the migratory labor estate; and Viet Nam, sharecropping. Paige uses theoretical concepts and typologies presented in the first half of his book to interpret the course of unrest in each of these four export sectors and buttresses his investigations of these cases with statistical analyses of cross-sectional and longitudinal (intranational) data. In short, he uses both classic case-oriented methods (interpreting cases in the light of theoretical concepts) and variable-oriented methods in his case studies. In this way, he is able to provide further verification for the soundness of his theory and, at the same time, show the theory's usefulness for interpreting specific cases.

Paige's work is theory-centered from beginning to end. The statistical examination of world patterns tests his theory in a manner entirely consistent with the dictates of the variable-oriented strategy. The case studies he appends to this global test enhance the statistical test. They provide a degree of assurance that the correlations observed are in some sense real and probably not the consequence of arbitrary measurement decisions. In Paige's combined strategy, the case studies are secondary. They are icing on the statistical cake. Thus, Paige's combined strategy is a variation of the variable-oriented strategy that incorporates features of the case-oriented approach.

THE TRANSITION FROM CAPITALISM TO SOCIALISM.   Stephens's combined strategy is very similar in form to Paige's. It includes both quantitative cross-national data analysis and detailed analyses of individual cases. Unlike Paige, however, in Stephens's work the two types of analysis are more integrated. Stephens pays close attention to deviant cases in his statistical analysis and uses these cases to aid the identification of omitted variables. He moves back and forth between statistical analysis and case analysis. Furthermore, in his comparative historical analyses he compares cases to each other. The cases do not exist simply to illustrate theory, as they do in Paige's work, but constitute an integral feature of the investigation. Paige appends case studies to his statistical analysis in order to validate and embellish it; Stephens, by contrast, conducts comparative case studies in order to deepen his investigation as a whole.

Stephens's main goal in his quantitative analysis is to explain variation in the development of the welfare state among seventeen "developed Western capitalist democracies" (1979 : 89). His major explanatory variables assess degree of working-class organization. This emphasis is inspired by Marxist theories emphasizing the importance of the working class in the transition from capitalism to socialism. Generally, Stephens finds strong support for the argument that variation in the strength of the working class explains variation in the development of the welfare state. For the seventeen countries he studies, the patterns are impressive, with Sweden and other Scandinavian countries at one end of the main axis of variation and the United States at the other.

The interplay of statistical and case analysis in Stephens's work is striking. Consider, for example, Stephens's (1979 : 100) discussion of the effect of the percentage of Catholics on welfare spending. Despite a negative zero-order relationship with welfare spending (consistent with expectations), it has a positive effect on welfare spending once the effect of years of socialist rule is controlled. Stephens (1979 : 100) examines the deviation of specific cases from the regression line both before and after the percentage of Catholics is added to the prediction equation and concludes that the relationship of Catholicism to welfare spending depends on context: "When Catholics are a center party and have a substantial base in the working class . . . then welfare state development will be encouraged. . . . The contrast between Belgium and Netherlands on the one hand and Germany on the other is a good example of this contrast."

Stephens's comparative case analysis examines four of his seventeen cases: Sweden, Great Britain, the United States, and France. These cases—the first three especially—are arrayed roughly along the main axis of variation evident in the statistical analysis. The case-oriented analysis, however, does not simply reproduce the statistical analysis. Essentially, the statistical analysis identifies the major explanatory variables without showing any concrete mechanisms or human agency. In other words, it shows that working-class organization is the main explanatory variable, but it does not show how or under what conditions working-class mobilization led to growth of the welfare state. The comparative analysis addresses this issue primarily by contrasting Sweden, the ideal-typic case (from Stephens's perspective), with three cases which depart from the Swedish case in varying degrees (Great Britain, moderately; the United States and France, substantially and in different ways). In this way Stephens is able to combine attention to structural factors (highlighted in the statistical analysis) with attention to historical factors and historical process.

The statistical and case-oriented analyses fit together relatively neatly because both are anchored by the same model, which is based ultimately on the Swedish case. The statistical analysis focuses on a single main axis of variation and deviations from this axis. The case-oriented analysis reproduces that axis in its use of Sweden as the ideal-typic case. Thus, Stephens's combination of case-oriented and variable-oriented techniques is more successful than either Paige's or Shorter and Tilly's because it uses an explicit model embodied in a specific case, Sweden, to orient both types of investigations. This feature orients Stephens's investigation more toward assessing generality (specifically, the generality of the Swedish social democratic model) than toward appreciating complexity and specificity, but considerable sensitivity to historical process is shown in the comparative case studies and the reader gains a strong sense of the diversity among advanced Western capitalist countries.

COMBINED STRATEGIES AND THE RELATION BETWEEN GOALS AND METHODS

The combined strategies presented above vary in the degree to which they successfully integrate case-oriented and variable-oriented approaches. Paige and Shorter and Tilly clearly are less successful than Stephens. Neither of the first two studies we have examined qualifies as a case-oriented *comparative* study. One simple signal of their noncomparative nature is the fact that neither study examines similar (or at least comparable) outcomes in different settings. Studies that address comparable outcomes across a range of cases usually must cope with multiple conjunctural causation in some way, and this type of examination is rare in the first two studies examined. (Paige does explore a few simple statistical interactions in some of his analyses; see, for example, his analysis of sharecropping in the section on global patterns.)

Recall that in classic comparative case studies such as Moore's *Social Origins of Dictatorship and Democracy*, a common finding is that a given outcome (say, the emergence of democratic political institutions) can result from several different causal conjunctures and that the same causal condition (say,

commercialization of agriculture) can have very different consequences, depending on context. The task of the historically oriented social scientist is to
unravel such apparent paradoxes (see Chapters 2 and 3).

In the first two combined strategies discussed above there is little need to
unravel paradox. Shorter and Tilly study only one case, France, and Paige,
in his case studies at least, examines only one example of each of four types
of agrarian systems. Thus, Shorter and Tilly pay some attention to conjunctural causation in the interpretive account of the course of strikes in
France, but because the analysis is not explicitly comparative, there is no
special interest in multiple conjunctural causation—there is no check on the
generalizability of the causal conjunctures they identify. In Paige's work, different causes produce different outcomes in the statistical analyses and in the
case studies, but each type of unrest results from a different cause or set of
causes. Again, there is no interest in multiple conjunctural causation, no explicit paradox to unravel. In some of his models and in some of his case
studies there are examples of interaction and conjunctural causation (as in
the treatment of military conjunctures in Angola and Viet Nam), but the
overall pattern is one of different causes explaining different outcomes, not
of different combinations of causes explaining the same outcome or similar
outcomes.

Stephens's study is much more successful at combining the two strategies,
and considerable attention is devoted to multiple and conjunctural causation.
However, the integration of the two strategies is made possible by the theoretical and methodological dominance of the Swedish case and therefore is
limited. Essentially, the statistical analyses show that countries most like
Sweden in terms of working-class mobilization and strength tend to have the
most developed and the most redistributive welfare states. The case studies
show different historical factors that account for different departures from
the Swedish case. Thus, Stephens addresses comparable outcomes in different settings in a restricted way, using the Swedish case to structure the entire
discussion. An analysis that did not treat any particular case as ideal typic
might show several different historical routes to the development of different types of welfare states.

Of course, research strategies should be evaluated only relative to stated
research goals, not relative to abstract notions concerning ideal comparative
work. Shorter and Tilly's primary goal was to understand and interpret the
nature and causes of strikes in France, especially since industrialization, and
to examine their relation to national political changes. Their analysis is cer-

tainly relevant to other advanced countries, but they carefully refrain from generalization—their goals are specific to France. Clearly, from this perspective, the strategy they selected was appropriate, perhaps exemplary in a paradigmatic sense.

In a similar vein, Paige's goal was to demonstrate his theory, to show that different ways of organizing agrarian life produce different, characteristic forms of agrarian unrest. In a sense, his only goal was to show that the typology he developed, based on income sources of cultivators and non-cultivators, works both at a global level and at a case-study level. He shows that it works at a global level by establishing correlations between types of agrarian structures and types of unrest; he shows that it works at a case-study level by using it as a basis for interpreting agrarian unrest in four export sectors. (In some of the case studies, however, the model works only in conjunction with political contextual variables not specified in the theoretical model.) From the perspective of goals, the methods Paige used were clearly appropriate, among the best that mainstream social science could offer.

Stephens's primary goal was to show the generalizability of the historical pattern of welfare state development evident in Sweden to other Western capitalist democracies. He builds a convincing case that the Swedish model is generalizable, and he shows further that the historical conditions highlighted by examination of the Swedish case are also important for understanding the experiences of other advanced countries. Again, from the perspective of goals, the overall design of the study cannot be faulted, and Stephens's implementation of the combined strategy comes closest to integrating the two approaches.

Still, it is possible to speculate that the *goals* of these studies were shaped to some degree by available methods. Consider, for example, Shorter and Tilly's chapter addressing comparative data. Essentially, this chapter consists of a brief examination of the changing shape of strikes (embracing number, average size, and average duration) in Western Europe and North America before and after World War II. In the course of this examination, Shorter and Tilly move toward a delineation of general patterns and suggest tentative assignments of countries to the patterns they identify. The exercise is incomplete, however, because the task of specifying the underlying commonalities that produce these different general patterns quickly gets out of hand. Strict application of the indirect method of difference (that is, identifying commonalities within types and consistent differences between types) is not attempted because the number of relevant causal conditions and the different combinations of causes is too great and the number of cases too few. Shorter and Tilly are left with only a general conclusion—that a common, but far from universal, pattern is for strikes to become larger and briefer, a pattern exemplified by France. Rather than attempting to unravel the complexities of the relations between the changing shape of industrial conflict and the nature of state formation in Western Europe and North America, they settle for a weaker statement of broad patterns.

Consider also Paige's statistical analysis of global patterns. His goal was simply to demonstrate his theory. The results of his analysis, while impressive from a statistical standpoint, leave many questions unanswered. For example, the correlation between the existence of decentralized sharecropping (coded as a presence/absence variable) and the log of number of revolutionary socialist events for agricultural export sectors is 0.51 (Paige 1975 : 106). This is a modest correlation, probably deflated somewhat by the presence/absence coding of the independent variable. However, it is still very far from perfect. Why is it that some decentralized sharecropping systems experienced high levels of revolutionary socialist events and others did not? Could it be that there are subtle differences among decentralized sharecropping systems (perhaps related to income sources of cultivators and noncultivators, perhaps not) that would account for these differences? Could it be that revolutionary socialist events occur only in agrarian systems experiencing some form of decolonization (or neocolonization)? And why did some of the other types of agrarian systems experience revolutionary socialist events? In short, what different combinations of agrarian (and political) conditions actually cause a high level of revolutionary socialist unrest?

Essentially, the problem is that Paige's independent variables (presence/absence of different types of agrarian systems) aggregates information about conditions and structures that separately (and in different combinations) may be relevant to revolutionary socialist unrest. It is impossible for the reader to disaggregate them into a form that would allow a more detailed examination of the link between agrarian conditions and revolutionary socialist unrest. Thus, there is a paradox—the correlation indicates that many decentralized sharecropping systems did not experience revolutionary socialist events and many other types of systems did—but it cannot be unraveled. The need for more detailed information on cases is obvious at this point, information that could be used to compare agricultural export sectors as wholes, as combinations of conditions.

It would be difficult, of course, to compare 135 agricultural export sectors with each other as wholes (9,045 comparisons) or even to do 135 case studies. Recognizing this problem (and the limitations of his correlational analysis), Paige presents detailed analyses of four representative export sectors. But is this sufficient? An analytic technique allowing a more global examination of complexity—of the different combinations of agrarian and other conditions associated with each type of unrest—would address the question of agrarian unrest more directly.

Again, this was not Paige's goal. He did not set out to unravel multiple conjunctural causation; he wanted simply to demonstrate his ideas. Similarly, Shorter and Tilly did not set out to unravel the complex links between the changing course of industrial conflict and the forging of contemporary Western polities. They focused on France. The point is simply that in both studies it is possible that certain avenues of investigation may have been blocked by method—by the inability of conventional methods to address a form of causal complexity that is common in comparative investigation of macrosocial phenomena. In the next section I describe ideal features of a broadly comparative research strategy, an approach that integrates aspects of variable-oriented and case-oriented methods.

ELEMENTS OF A SYNTHETIC STRATEGY

What features should a synthetic strategy possess? First, it should be capable of addressing large numbers of cases. The primary weakness of the case-oriented strategy is that it is open to the charge of particularism. The conclusions of case-oriented studies are typically based on few cases. Social scientists who read these studies routinely ask: Are these cases typical? Do they embrace the entire range of relevant variation? Shorter and Tilly's *Strikes in France* is open to this criticism. Their comparative data, in fact, suggest that France is not typical. Even Moore's *Social Origins of Dictatorship and Democracy* is vulnerable to this attack. He claims that his analysis is relevant only to big or important countries, not to all countries or to all instances of political modernization. A proper synthetic strategy should provide an avenue of escape from this criticism. At a minimum, it should allow investigators who wish to protect themselves from this charge to examine more than a few cases.

Second, a synthetic strategy should embody as much of the strict comparative logic of experimental design as possible (see Chapters 1, 2, and 3).

This logic is a key feature of case-oriented comparative study. It is apparent in this strategy's concern for combinations of conditions and in its allowance for complex, conjunctural causation. According to the metatheory of this strategy, social causes often modify the effects of other social causes, sometimes mutating and transforming their impact. Such causal complexity cannot be captured easily in statistical analyses, especially in additive models. Only an approach that allows consideration of different combinations of conditions will suffice. This is the second major feature that a proper synthetic strategy should exhibit.

These first two features are essential; however, there are additional features that are also important. A synthetic strategy should allow investigators to formulate parsimonious explanations. In some types of investigation parsimony is not desirable. For example, full appreciation of the variety of party systems in contemporary democracies does not necessarily call for a parsimonious strategy. In general, to the extent that knowledge of complexity is desired, a parsimonious strategy is more of a burden than a blessing. In the social sciences, however, parsimony typically is preferred to extensive knowledge of complexity. To be consistent with one of the central goals of social science, therefore, a synthetic strategy should be capable of producing relatively parsimonious explanations. In essence, this means that a synthetic strategy should be capable of data reduction—of simplifying complexity in a theoretically guided manner.

A synthetic strategy should also be analytic. That is, it should provide a way for investigators to specify and study the major features of social units and social processes, the parts that combine in different ways to produce different wholes. Analysis entails breaking wholes into parts. It is by understanding how parts fit together that social scientists are able to understand wholes. Social science is not, at least not yet, a science of essences; analysis, breaking wholes into parts, remains important. In purely variable-oriented investigations, analysis proceeds by examining the relations between parts in isolation from wholes. In case-oriented studies, by contrast, the whole predominates over the parts, shaping the understanding and interpretation of each separate element. This is especially true in investigations where the goal is to interpret the uniqueness, the particularity, of a case or set of cases. In opposition to these extremes, a synthetic strategy should allow analysis of parts in a way that does not obscure wholes. In short, it should provide a basis for qualitative, holistic analysis, the comparison of wholes as combinations or configurations of parts.

A synthetic strategy should also allow consideration of alternative explanations. One weakness of case-oriented studies is the fact that they are very private products; they contradict the communal norms of scientific investigation (Merton 1973). A case-oriented investigator labors in isolation to produce a study which, in the end, bears his or her mark. Typically, a case-oriented study elaborates the ideas and theories of the investigator with data that are not generally known or accessible to other investigators, and often only perfunctory consideration of alternative explanations and arguments is offered. In essence, case-oriented analyses usually stack the deck in favor of the preferred theory. The variable-oriented strategy, by contrast, is conservative by design. Favored theories are pitted against alternatives and forced to compete in the struggle to explain variation. While the variable-oriented strategy is more consistent with the norms of scientific investigation, especially those borrowed from the natural sciences, its conservative bias discourages interpretive analysis. Theories win or lose; only rarely are they used to understand events. A synthetic strategy should provide a way to test alternative arguments and at the same time encourage the use of theory as a basis for interpretation. After all, the goals of social science are to test theories—to reject unsupportable ideas—but also to advance the collective understanding of common origins and possible common destinies.

In short, the ideal synthetic strategy should integrate the best features of the case-oriented approach with the best features of the variable-oriented approach. This integration would allow investigators to address questions relevant to many cases in a way that does not contradict either the complexity of social causation or the variety of empirical social phenomena. The key to a proper synthetic strategy is the idea of qualitative comparative analysis—the notion of comparing wholes as configurations of parts. This is the *via media* between complexity and generality, between the radically analytic variable-oriented strategy and the highly personalized case-oriented strategy.

Qualitative comparison of cases is not easily accomplished with traditional statistical methods based on linear algebra. In the next chapter I present an alternative algebraic basis for comparative analysis. Specifically, I show how Boolean algebra can be used as a basis for analyzing multiple conjunctural causation.

6

A Boolean Approach to
Qualitative Comparison: Basic Concepts

An explicit algebraic basis for qualitative comparison exists in Boolean algebra. Also known as the algebra of logic and as the algebra of sets, Boolean algebra was developed in the mid-nineteenth century by George Boole. It is not necessary to understand Boolean algebra in its entirety in order to comprehend its uses in comparative social science. The Boolean principles used in qualitative comparative analysis are quite simple. They are easy to grasp because they are consistent with simple logical principles common to many types of social scientific investigation. To a slightly lesser extent they are also consistent with everyday experience.

This chapter outlines basic features of Boolean algebra relevant to qualitative comparison. Although it is not an introduction to Boolean algebra, which is beyond the scope of this book, all relevant features of Boolean algebra are presented. This chapter also describes the Boolean algorithms that are used to compare cases holistically and presents simple, hypothetical examples. These algorithms are based on the work of electrical engineers who developed them in the 1950s to simplify switching circuits. As I hope to show, these are not mechanical procedures—despite their origins. There is an important element of investigator input, what electrical engineers would call engineering art, at virtually every stage of Boolean-based qualitative comparison. Chapter 7 presents advanced principles of Boolean algebra, and Chapter 8 presents examples of the application of these procedures to several data sets.

It is important to point out that the qualitative comparative method presented in this and subsequent chapters uses Boolean algebra, but it is not limited to this algebraic system. It is possible to mimic many of the basic algorithmic principles discussed with more conventional techniques, and it is possible to apply some of these alternative techniques to interval-scale variables. Thus, the ideas presented in these chapters are not limited to dichotomous social data (such as presence/absence of structures or events) or to a narrowly Boolean (that is, logical) formulation. A strictly Boolean approach is presented because the principles of qualitative comparison are much easier to grasp and to apply when formulated in this manner.

BASIC FEATURES OF BOOLEAN ALGEBRA

There are ten aspects of Boolean algebra that are essential to its use in social science. These are presented in rough sequence here, with more difficult concepts following simpler concepts. Whenever possible, applications to hypothetical social data are supplied.

USE OF BINARY DATA.   There are two conditions or states in Boolean algebra: true (or present) and false (or absent). These two states are represented in base 2: 1 indicates presence; 0 indicates absence. The typical Boolean-based comparative analysis addresses the presence/absence conditions under which a certain outcome is obtained (that is, is true). Thus, in a Boolean analysis of social data all variables, independent and dependent, must be nominal-scale measures. Interval-scale measures are transformed into multicategory nominal-scale measures. Nominal-scale measures with more than two categories are represented with several binary variables.

While these procedures entail some loss of information, the loss typically is not great. In many comparative studies this restriction does not pose a major obstacle because many phenomena of interest to comparativists, both causes and outcomes, are already nominal-scale measures. They are qualitative phenomena, such as the presence or absence of events, processes, and structures, that are difficult to measure on interval scales. In Barrington Moore's (1966) study, for example, the main "variables" were qualitative distinctions such as the presence or absence of communal peasant villages in certain countries or regions. While interval-scale measures of some of the phenomena of interest to comparativists are sometimes available, meaningful transformation of such measures into multicategory nominal-scale variables can be achieved by incorporating substantive and theoretical criteria.

USE OF TRUTH TABLE TO REPRESENT DATA. In order to use Boolean algebra as a technique of qualitative comparison, it is necessary to reconstruct a raw data matrix as a truth table. The idea behind a truth table is simple. Once the data have been recoded into nominal-scale variables and represented in binary form (as 1's and 0's), it is necessary only to sort the data into their different combinations of values on the independent variables. Each logical combination of values on the independent variables is represented as one row of the truth table. Once this part of the truth table is constructed, each row is assigned an output value (a score of 1 or 0 on the dependent variable) based on the scores of the cases which share that combination of input values (that combination of scores on the independent variables). Thus, both the different combinations of input values (independent variables) and their associated output values (the dependent variable) are summarized in a truth table.

Truth tables have as many rows as there are logically possible combinations of values on the causal variables. If there are four binary independent variables, for example, the truth table will contain $2^4 = 16$ rows, one for each logically possible combination of four presence/absence independent variables. The truth table for a moderate-sized data set with four binary independent variables and one binary dependent variable (with $1 =$ present and $0 =$ absent) is shown in Table 3. (In all, this truth table would have sixteen rows.) Technically, there is no reason to include the frequency of each combination as part of the truth table. These values are included in the examples to remind the reader that each row is not a single case but a summary of all the cases with a certain combination of input values. In this respect, a row of a truth table is like a cell from a multiway cross-classification of several categorical independent variables.

Note that the outcome variable must be either 1 or 0, not an average or a probability. This requirement may present problems to the extent that clear tendencies are not evident in the data. In the first row of the hypothetical truth table (cases scoring 0 on all four causes, X_1 to X_4), for example, if the cases were evenly divided between an outcome of 0 and an outcome of 1 (that is, four of each), it would have been difficult to assign an output value to this row of the truth table. There are several possible solutions to this

TABLE 3: Representative Truth Table with Four Causal Conditions

Condition				Outcome	Number of
X_1	X_2	X_3	X_4	Y	Instances
0	0	0	0	0	8
0	0	0	1	0	6
0	0	1	0	1	10
0	0	1	1	0	5
0	1	0	0	1	13
0	1	0	1	0	7
0	1	1	0	1	11
0	1	1	1	1	5
1	0	0	0	1	9
1	0	0	1	1	3
1	0	1	0	0	12
1	0	1	1	0	23
1	1	0	0	0	15
1	1	0	1	1	5
1	1	1	0	0	8
1	1	1	1	1	6

problem, which are addressed in detail in Chapter 7. For the moment, assume that the data in the examples are unusually straightforward and that no contradictory rows exist. The important concept is that Boolean techniques of qualitative comparison use truth tables, which are constructed from binary raw data on cases sorted into their different combinations of values on the causal variables.

In a Boolean analysis, the number of instances of each combination of causal conditions does not enter directly into any computations. In other words, frequency criteria are not as important as they are in statistical analysis. This practice is consistent with a focus on types of situations (that is, rows of the truth table) as the basic analytic unit. This does not mean that frequency criteria cannot or should not be incorporated in any way. There are several possible ways to incorporate frequency criteria (see, for example, the third application in Chapter 8). One simple way to incorporate such criteria would be to establish cutoff values for rows of the truth table. For example, an investigator might decide that if there are not at least four instances of a certain combination of input values, as in row 2 of the hypothetical truth table (Table 3) where there are only three, then that combination of values should be excluded from consideration. Of course, there are simple statistical rules that can be used for such decisions which certainly should be applied when appropriate. (Ragin and others 1984 present one rudimentary technique.)

BOOLEAN ADDITION. In Boolean algebra, if $A + B = Z$, and $A = 1$ and $B = 1$, then $Z = 1$. In other words, $1 + 1 = 1$. The basic idea in Boolean addition is that if any of the additive terms is satisfied (present), then the outcome is true (occurs). Addition in Boolean algebra is equivalent to the logical operator OR. (In this discussion uppercase OR is used to indicate logical OR.) Thus, the statement $A + B = Z$ becomes: if A equals 1 OR B equals 1, then Z equals 1.

The best way to think of this principle is in logical terms, not arithmetically. For example, there might be several things a person could do to lose his or her job. It does not matter how many of these things the person does. If the employee does any one (or all) of them, he or she will be fired. Doing two of them will not cause one employee to be more fired than another employee who does only one of them. Fired is fired, a truly qualitative state. This example succinctly illustrates the nature of Boolean addition: satisfy any one of the additive conditions and the expected outcome follows. This aspect of Boolean addition is very useful in social scientific analysis, especially qualitative comparison, although its value is not generally recognized.

Consider the collapse of military regimes. Assume that there are three general conditions that cause military regimes to fall: sharp conflict between older and younger military officers (A), death of a powerful dictator (B), or CIA dissatisfaction with the regime (C). Any one of these three conditions may be sufficient to prompt a collapse. The truth table for a number of such regimes in different countries is shown in Table 4 (with 1 = present and 0 = absent). Each combination of causes produces either regime failure or an absence of regime failure—there are no contradictory rows.

With uppercase letters indicating the presence of a condition and lowercase letters indicating its absence (a convention used throughout this discussion), the "simplified" Boolean equation

$$F = A + B + C$$

TABLE 4: Hypothetical Truth Table Showing Three Causes of Regime Failure

Condition			Regime Failure	Number of
A	B	C	F	Instances
0	0	0	0	9
1	0	0	1	2
0	1	0	1	3
0	0	1	1	1
1	1	0	1	2
1	0	1	1	1
0	1	1	1	1
1	1	1	1	3

A = Conflict between older and younger military officers
B = Death of a powerful dictator
C = CIA dissatisfaction with the regime

expresses the relation between the three conditions and regime failure simply and elegantly for both negative and positive instances. Simply stated: if any one (or any two or all three) of these conditions obtains, then the regime will fall.

It would be difficult to achieve this same directness in a statistical analysis because a linear, additive combination of these three presence/absence variables would predict that cases with more than one of the three conditions present should somehow experience more of a regime failure. But a regime either falls or it does not (assuming the investigator has applied the relevant criteria correctly and consistently); the distinction is qualitative.

In order to model these data with statistical methods, many more cases would have to be found and added to the set. Assuming this, the investigator might apply discriminant analysis or some type of log-linear analysis to the data. The goal of the discriminant analysis would be to estimate a linear, arithmetic combination of causal variables in a way that maximizes the separation of the scores of predefined groups on a "discriminant function" while minimizing within-group variation on these scores. To use this technique effectively it would be necessary to include terms modeling the statistical interaction between the causal variables (with negative coefficients) as predictors to correct for the fact that when two or more relevant conditions are present, the score on the discriminant function should remain constant (that is, be equal to 1) within the regime failure group. Similarly, a log-linear analysis of this hypothetical (dramatically enlarged) data set would show interaction. Thus, a simple (and clear) model from a logical (that is, Boolean) point of view would be awkward to model statistically.

A statistician's immediate response to this problem would be to argue that the investigator should use a different dependent variable—perhaps number of deaths associated with the collapse of each regime, a convenient interval-scale dependent variable. But this would be a different analysis and a different question. It would be an analysis of the bloodiness of regime changes, not of the conditions that prompt the collapse of military regimes.

Historical and comparative social scientists are often interested in outcomes of this type—events and formations that are best viewed as historically emergent and therefore qualitative. It is difficult to transform such qualitative occurrences into meaningful interval-scale dependent variables suitable for conventional multivariate statistical analysis. This is not to say, of course, that statistical methods cannot be applied to categorical dependent variables. The point is simply that the Boolean model is more consistent with how we often think about and understand qualitative phenomena.

BOOLEAN MULTIPLICATION.   Boolean multiplication differs substantially from normal multiplication. Boolean multiplication is relevant because the typical social science application of Boolean algebra concerns the process of simplifying expressions known as "sums of products." A product is a specific combination of causal conditions. With uppercase letters indicating presence and lowercase letters indicating absence, the data on collapsed military regimes from Table 4 can be represented in "primitive" (that is, unreduced) sums-of-products form as follows:

$$F = Abc + aBc + abC + ABc + AbC + aBC + ABC$$

Each of the seven terms represents a combination of causal conditions found in at least one instance of regime failure. The different terms are products because they represent intersections of conditions (conjunctures of causes and absences of causes). The equation shows the different primitive combinations of conditions that are linked to the collapse of military regimes.

Boolean multiplication, like Boolean addition, is not arithmetic. The expression Abc does not mean that the value of A (1) is multiplied by the value of B (0) and by the value of C (0) to produce a result value of 0. It means simply that a presence of A is combined with an absence of B and an absence of C. The total situation, $F = Abc$, occurs in the data twice. This conjunctural character of Boolean multiplication shapes the interpretation of the primitive sums-of-products equation presented above: F (regime failure) occurs if any of seven combinations of three causes is obtained. In Boolean algebra, therefore, addition indicates logical OR and multiplication indicates logical AND. The three causes are ANDed together in different ways to indicate different empirical configurations. These intersections are ORed together to form an unreduced, sums-of-products equation describing the different combinations of the three causes linked to regime failure.

COMBINATORIAL LOGIC.   Boolean analysis is combinatorial by design. In the analysis of regime failures presented above, it appears from casual inspection of only the first four rows of the truth table (Table 4) that if any one of the three causes is present, then the regime will collapse. While it is tempting to take this shortcut, the route taken by Boolean analysis is much more exacting of the data. This is because the absence of a cause has the same logical status as the presence of a cause in Boolean analysis. As noted above, Boolean multiplication indicates that presence and absence conditions are combined, that they intersect.

Consider the second row of the truth table (Table 4), which describes the two instances of military regime failure linked to causal configuration Abc. Simple inspection suggests that in this case F (regime failure) resulted from the first cause, A. But notice that if the investigator had information on only this row of the truth table, and not on any of the other instances of regime failure, he or she *might* conclude that A causes F only if causes B and C are absent. This is what the Abc combination indicates. This row by itself does not indicate whether A would cause F in the presence of B or C or both. All the researcher knows from these two instances of Abc is that for A to cause F, it may be necessary for the other conditions (B and C) to be absent. From a Boolean perspective, it is entirely plausible that in the presence of one or both of these other conditions (say, configuration AbC), F may not result. To return to the original designations, it may be that in the presence of CIA meddling (C), conflict between junior and senior officers (A) will dissipate as the two factions unite to oppose the attempt by outsiders to dictate events.

To push this argument further, assume the investigator had knowledge of only the first four rows of the truth table. The data would support the idea that the presence of any one of the three conditions causes F, but again the data might indicate that A causes F only when B and C are absent (Abc), B causes F only when A and C are absent (aBc), and so on. A strict application of combinatorial logic requires that these limitations be placed on conclusions drawn from a limited variety of cases. (Chapter 7 discusses how these restrictions can be addressed.)

This feature of combinatorial logic is consistent with the idea that cases, especially their causally relevant features, should be viewed holistically. The holistic character of the Boolean approach is consistent with the orientation of qualitative scholars in comparative social science who examine different causes in context. When the second row of the truth table (Table 4) is examined, it is not interpreted as instances of F caused by A but as instances of F caused by Abc. Thus, in Boolean-based qualitative comparison, causes are not viewed in isolation but always within the context of the presence and absence of other causally relevant conditions.

BOOLEAN MINIMIZATION. The restrictive character of combinatorial logic seems to indicate that the Boolean approach simply compounds complexity on top of complexity. This is not the case. There are simple and straightforward rules for simplifying complexity—for reducing primitive expressions and formulating more succinct Boolean statements. The most fundamental of these rules is:

If two Boolean expressions differ in only one causal condition yet produce the same outcome, then the causal condition that distinguishes the two expressions can be considered irrelevant and can be removed to create a simpler, combined expression.

Essentially this minimization rule allows the investigator to take two Boolean expressions that differ in only one term and produce a combined expression. For example, Abc and ABc, which both produce outcome F, differ only in B; all other elements are identical. The minimization rule stated above allows the replacement of these two terms with a single, simpler expression: Ac. In other words, the comparison of these two rows, Abc and ABc, as wholes indicates that in instances of Ac, the value of B is irrelevant. Cause B may be either present or absent; F will still occur.

The logic of this simple data reduction parallels the logic of experimental design (Chapter 2). Only one causal condition, B, varies and no difference in outcome is detected (because both Abc and ABc are instances of F). According to the logic of experimental design, B is irrelevant to F in the presence of

Ac (that is, holding these two conditions constant). Thus, the process of Boolean minimization mimics the logic of experimental design. It is a straightforward operationalization of the logic of the ideal social scientific comparison.

This process of logical minimization is conducted in a bottom-up fashion until no further stepwise reduction of Boolean expressions is possible. Consider again the data on military regime failures presented above. Each of the rows with one cause present and two absent can be combined with rows with two causes present and one absent because all these rows have the same outcome (*F*) and each pair differs in only one causal condition:

Abc combines with *ABc* to produce *Ac*.

Abc combines with *AbC* to produce *Ab*.

aBc combines with *ABc* to produce *Bc*.

aBc combines with *aBC* to produce *aB*.

abC combines with *AbC* to produce *bC*.

abC combines with *aBC* to produce *aC*.

Similarly, each of the rows with two causes present and one absent can be combined with the row with all three present:

ABc combines with *ABC* to produce *AB*.

AbC combines with *ABC* to produce *AC*.

aBC combines with *ABC* to produce *BC*.

Further reduction is possible. Note that the reduced terms produced in the first round can be combined with the reduced terms produced in the second round to produce even simpler expressions:

Ab combines with *AB* to produce *A*.

Ac combines with *AC* to produce *A*.

aB combines with *AB* to produce *B*.

Bc combines with *BC* to produce *B*.

aC combines with *AC* to produce *C*.

bC combines with *BC* to produce *C*.

Although tedious, this simple process of minimization produces the final, reduced Boolean equation:

$$F = A + B + C$$

True enough, this was obvious from simple inspection of the entire truth table, but the problem presented was chosen for its simplicity. The example directly illustrates key features of Boolean minimization. It is bottom-up (that is, inductively oriented). It seeks to identify ever wider sets of conditions (that is, simpler combinations of causal conditions) for which an outcome is true. And it is experiment-like in its focus on pairs of configurations differing in only one cause.

IMPLICATION AND THE USE OF "PRIME IMPLICANTS."   A further Boolean concept that needs to be introduced is the concept of implication. A Boolean expression is said to imply another if the membership of the second term is a subset of the membership of the first. For example, A implies Abc because A embraces all the members of Abc (that is, Abc is a subset of A). This concept is best understood by example. If A indicates economically dependent countries, B indicates the presence of heavy industry, and C indicates centrally coordinated economies, A embraces all dependent countries while Abc embraces all dependent countries that lack both centrally coordinated economies and heavy industry. Clearly the membership of Abc is included in the membership of A. Thus, A implies Abc.

The concept of implication, while obvious, provides an important tool for minimizing primitive sums-of-products expressions. Consider the hypothetical truth table shown in Table 5, which summarizes data on three causal conditions thought to affect the success of strikes already in progress (S): a booming market for the product produced by the strikers (A), the threat of sympathy strikes by workers in associated industries (B), and the existence of a large strike fund (C).

The Boolean equation for S (successful strikes) showing unreduced (primitive) Boolean expressions is

$$S = AbC + aBc + ABc + ABC$$

The first step in the Boolean analysis of these data is to attempt to combine as many compatible rows of the truth table as possible. (Note that this

TABLE 5: Hypothetical Truth Table Showing Three Causes of Successful Strikes

Condition			Success	Frequency
A	B	C	S	
1	0	1	1	6
0	1	0	1	5
1	1	0	1	2
1	1	1	1	3
1	0	0	0	9
0	0	1	0	6
0	1	1	0	3
0	0	0	0	4

A = Booming product market
B = Threat of sympathy strikes
C = Large strike fund

part of the minimization process uses rows with an output value of 1—
strike succeeded.) This first phase of the minimization of the truth table
produces the following partially minimized Boolean equation, which in
effect turns a primitive Boolean equation with four three-variable terms
into an equation with three two-variable terms:

ABC combines with AbC to produce AC.

ABC combines with ABc to produce AB.

ABc combines with aBc to produce Bc.

$S = AC + AB + Bc$

Product terms such as those in the preceding equation which are produced using this simple minimization rule—combine rows that differ on
only one cause if they have the same output values—are called prime implicants. Usually, each prime implicant covers (that is, implies) several primitive expressions in the truth table. In the partially minimized equation given
above, for example, prime implicant AC covers two primitive Boolean expressions listed in the truth table: ABC and AbC.

This partially reduced Boolean expression illustrates a common finding in
Boolean analysis: often there are more reduced expressions (prime implicants) than are needed to cover all the original primitive expressions. Prime
implicant AB implies primitive terms ABC and ABc, for example, yet these

two primitive terms are also covered by AC and Bc, respectively. Thus, AB may be redundant from a purely logical point of view; it may not be an essential prime implicant. In order to determine which prime implicants are logically essential, a minimization device known as a prime implicant chart is used. Minimization of the prime implicant chart is an optional, second phase of Boolean minimization.

Briefly stated, the goal of this second phase of the minimization process is to "cover" as many of the primitive Boolean expressions as possible with a logically minimal number of prime implicants. This objective derives from a straightforward desire for parsimony. The prime implicant chart maps the links between prime implicants and primitive expressions. The prime implicant chart describing these links in the data on strike outcomes is presented in Table 6. Simple inspection indicates that the smallest number of prime implicants needed to cover all of the original primitive expressions is two. (For very complex prime implicant charts, sophisticated computer algorithms are needed; see Mendelson 1970, Roth 1975, and McDermott 1985.) Prime implicants AC and Bc cover all four primitive Boolean expressions. Analysis of the prime implicant chart, therefore, leads to the final reduced Boolean expression containing only the logically essential prime implicants:

$$S = AC + Bc$$

This equation states simply that successful strikes occur when there is a booming market for the product produced by the workers AND a large strike fund (AC) or when there is the threat of sympathy strikes by workers in associated industries combined with a low strike fund (Bc). (Perhaps the threat of sympathy strikes is taken seriously only when the striking workers badly need the support of other workers.)

TABLE 6: Prime Implicant Chart Showing Coverage of Original Terms by Prime Implicants (Hypothetical Strike Data)

		Primitive Expressions			
		ABC	AbC	ABc	aBc
Prime Implicants	AC	×	×		
	AB	×		×	
	Bc			×	×

These simple procedures allow the investigator to derive a logically minimal equation describing the different combinations of conditions associated with a certain outcome. The final, reduced equation shows the two (logically minimal) combinations of conditions that cause successful strikes and thus provides an explicit statement of multiple conjunctural causation.

Note that this final phase of Boolean minimization, use of the prime implicant chart, is used only when the investigator seeks a *logically* minimal equation (that is, maximum logical parsimony). In some analyses the determination of prime implicants may be the endpoint of the Boolean analysis. If, for example, the investigator's theory emphasized combination AB (the coincidence of a booming market and the threat of sympathy strikes) as an important cause of successful strikes, the fact that AB never exists in a "pure" form (that is, in the absence of either AC or Bc) might be considered irrelevant, and the cases that combine AB with either AC or Bc might be considered "overdetermined" (and possibly more interpretable) according to this reasoning and deserve special attention. The important point here is that in all applications of these procedures there is an element of investigator input that is crucial. The techniques should not be used mechanically. The issue of parsimony is addressed in more detail in Chapters 7 and 8 where I examine the use of theory to evaluate the results of Boolean analysis.

The hypothetical analysis presented here shows the major steps in using Boolean techniques to unravel complexity: (1) construct the truth table, (2) determine the prime implicants, and (3) use the prime implicant chart to select the essential prime implicants (if maximum parsimony is desired). The truth table shows primitive expressions. An equation with prime implicants is a partially reduced Boolean expression. The equation that results from use of the prime implicant chart is a logically minimal Boolean expression.

USE OF DE MORGAN'S LAW.   Once a truth table has been minimized and the different combinations of conditions associated with an outcome have been determined, it is often useful to assess the combinations of conditions associated with the absence of an outcome (such as unsuccessful strikes in the example above). Rather than start from the very beginning and construct and minimize a new truth table, it is possible to apply De Morgan's Law to the solution already derived for positive outcomes to obtain the solution for negative outcomes.

The application of De Morgan's Law is straightforward. Consider the solution to the hypothetical analysis of successful strikes presented above: $S = AC + Bc$. Elements that are coded present in the reduced equation (say, A in the term AC) are recoded to absent, and elements that are coded absent (say, c in the term Bc) are recoded to present. Next, logical AND is recoded to logical OR, and logical OR is recoded to logical AND. Applying these two rules, $S = AC + Bc$ becomes

$$s = (a + c)(b + C)$$
$$= ab + aC + bc$$

According to this equation, strikes fail when (1) the market for the relevant product is not booming AND there is no serious threat of sympathy strikes, (2) the market for a product is not booming AND there is a large strike fund, OR (3) there is no threat of sympathy strikes AND only a small strike fund. (The combination aC—nonbooming market and large strike fund, which seems contradictory—may suggest an economic downturn after a period of stability. In this situation a shutdown might be welcomed by management.) De Morgan's Law thus provides a convenient shortcut for minimizing negative instances. It can also be used in conjunction with advanced Boolean techniques discussed in Chapter 7.

NECESSARY AND SUFFICIENT CAUSES.   An additional aspect of the Boolean approach to consider is the relation between the results of Boolean minimization and necessary and sufficient causes in social research. A cause is defined as necessary if it must be present for a certain outcome to occur. A cause is defined as sufficient if by itself it can produce a certain outcome. This distinction is meaningful only in the context of theoretical perspectives. No cause is necessary, for example, independent of a theory that specifies it as a relevant cause. Neither necessity nor sufficiency exists independently of theories that propose causes.

Necessity and sufficiency are usually considered jointly because all combinations of the two are meaningful. A cause is both necessary and sufficient if it is the only cause that produces an outcome and it is singular (that is, not a combination of causes). A cause is sufficient but not necessary if it is capable of producing the outcome but is not the only cause with this capability. A cause is necessary but not sufficient if it is capable of producing an outcome in combination with other causes and appears in all such combinations.

Finally, a cause is neither necessary nor sufficient if it appears only in a sub-set of the combinations of conditions that produce an outcome. In all, there are four categories of causes (formed from the cross-tabulation of the presence/absence of sufficiency against the presence/absence of necessity).

In contrast to the results of most types of statistical analysis, the results of Boolean analysis are easy to interpret in terms of necessity and sufficiency. Consider the following hypothetical:

$$S = AC + Bc \qquad \text{(No cause is either necessary or sufficient.)}$$

None of the four causal conditions in the equation (A, B, C, c) is either necessary or sufficient because all terms contain combinations of causes, and no causal condition appears in every term. If, instead, the final equation had been

$$S = AC + BC \qquad \text{(C is necessary but not sufficient.)}$$

it would have been possible to conclude that C is a necessary but not sufficient condition because it appears in every term but never by itself. Other examples showing other patterns of necessary and sufficient causation are

$$S = AC \qquad \text{(Both A and C are necessary but not sufficient.)}$$

$$S = A + Bc \qquad \text{(A is sufficient but not necessary.)}$$

$$S = B \qquad \text{(B is both necessary and sufficient.)}$$

These examples are very simple, but they show clearly that the Boolean approach is highly compatible with the vocabulary of necessary and sufficient causation. This feature enhances its value as a tool for qualitative comparative analysis, especially in studies examining a variety of cases experiencing the same or similar outcomes.

FACTORING BOOLEAN EXPRESSIONS.   Often it is useful to factor the results of Boolean analysis. Boolean factoring does not differ dramatically from standard algebraic factoring. For example, the Boolean statement

$$S = AB + AC + AD$$

can be factored to show that A is a necessary condition:

$$S = A(B + C + D)$$

Factoring is useful not only to show which conditions are necessary; it also identifies conditions that are causally equivalent. In the example given above, for instance, it is clear that conditions B, C, and D are causally equivalent (in combination with A) with respect to outcome S.

Factoring can also be used to clarify an equation, even when factoring the equation does not simplify it. For example, an investigator might find the following equation for S:

$$S = abc + AbC + abd + E$$

Theory might stress the contrary effects of A in different contexts, and the results seem to support this emphasis. In some contexts A must be present for S to occur; in others it must be absent. The equation can be factored in a way that highlights condition A in its presence and absence states:

$$S = a(bc + bd + E) + A(bC + E)$$

The equation shows which contexts require A to be present for S to occur and which contexts require A to be absent. Note that condition E appears in both sets. Because this second use of factoring does not simplify an equation, but clarifies it according to theoretical criteria, it is better to distinguish it by labeling it "theoretical factoring."

SUMMARY

The brief overview of Boolean techniques presented in this chapter illustrates some of the key features of the Boolean approach. It is holistic in its orientation toward cases because it views them in terms of combinations of values and compares cases with different combinations holistically. This feature of Boolean based qualitative comparison makes it an ideal instrument for identifying patterns of multiple conjunctural causation. The approach has a strong inductive element (which mimics case-oriented research) because it proceeds from the bottom up, simplifying complexity in a methodical, stepwise manner. It starts with a bias toward complexity—every logically possible combination of values is examined—and simplifies this complexity through experiment-like contrasts—procedures which approximate the logic of the ideal social scientific comparison. Finally, it is highly compatible with the vocabulary of necessary and sufficient causation, a feature that enhances its value for assessing the limits of social scientific generalizations.

This chapter leaves many basic questions unanswered, however. For example, what should an investigator do if some of the logically possible combinations of values on the independent variables do not exist? As noted in Chapter 2, this is a crucial question because naturally occurring data almost never display patterns allowing experiment-like comparisons. This and related issues are examined in Chapter 7.

7

Extensions of Boolean Methods of Qualitative Comparison

The hypothetical examples used in Chapter 6 to introduce Boolean techniques of qualitative comparison were unrealistically straightforward. Their simplicity eased the task of presenting basic Boolean principles but left many important issues unaddressed. This chapter also uses hypothetical data, but the examples are more complex. These hypothetical data come much closer to the empirical examples used in Chapter 8 to illustrate various applications of Boolean methods. Thus, this chapter bridges Chapters 6 and 8.

Several key issues were skirted in Chapter 6. The most important of these is one of the issues that motivated the development of Boolean techniques in the first place—the fact that naturally occurring data lack sufficient variety to allow experiment-like comparative analyses (see Chapters 2 and 3). As noted previously, techniques of statistical control were developed in part to address this problem of limited diversity. Boolean techniques respond to this same problem, but in a dramatically different way. Statistical techniques are able to approximate experiment-like comparisons by making (sometimes strained and unrealistic) assumptions about the nature of social causation. The Boolean approach seeks to avoid these assumptions and allows maximum causal complexity, at least initially. The Boolean approach to the problem of limited diversity is to incorporate the question of diversity directly into the analysis. This strategy is explained in detail in the first major section below.

Another important issue skirted in Chapter 6 is the problem of "contra-dictory rows." To construct a truth table, cases are sorted into their different combinations of values on the independent variables to form rows of the truth table, and then each row is assigned an output value—a score of 1 or 0 on the dependent variable. If clear tendencies are not apparent among the cases with the same combination of input values, then it is difficult to deter-mine the appropriate score for the dependent variable (the output value of the row). This problem is addressed in the second major section below.

A third issue concerns evaluating theoretical arguments. The rudimen-tary material presented in Chapter 6 left the false impression that theory enters into Boolean-based comparative analysis only in the selection of causal conditions and the construction of the truth table. From there on, the process appears to be relatively inductive. In fact, theoretical arguments about causal combinations can be incorporated into Boolean analysis. The third major section of this chapter outlines procedures for evaluating theo-retically based causal arguments. These techniques illustrate the flexibility of the Boolean approach and its compatibility with the goals of theory testing and theory building.

The final section of this chapter summarizes major features of the Boolean approach and evaluates it relative to ideal features of a synthetic strategy outlined in Chapter 5.

THE PROBLEM OF LIMITED DIVERSITY

Social scientists have a love-hate relationship with the fact that naturally oc-curring social phenomena display limited diversity. On the one hand, as pre-viously noted, limited diversity places severe constraints on possibilities for testing causal arguments. This is what makes comparative social science a challenge. On the other hand, however, social phenomena are limited in their diversity for very good reasons. The fact that all U.S. presidents have been white males, for example, is an obviously meaningful instance of lim-ited diversity. The fact that there are no non-Catholic South American countries is both meaningful and historically interpretable; it is not an un-fortunate accident that confounds the work of scholars who study Latin America. While such restrictions on diversity pose clear obstacles to assess-ing social causation, they also constitute profound testimony to the social forces that have shaped the modern world. The tendency for features of cases to be confounded and to clump into interpretable combinations is as much the stuff of social science as attempts to construct exhaustive experiment-like comparisons of causal conditions. That only a subset of the logically possible combinations of features of cases exists is prima facie evidence of a socially constructed order.

Because of limited diversity, statements about causation (in the absence of simplifying assumptions) are necessarily restricted to the combinations of causally relevant conditions that actually exist. If an analysis were to show, for example, that rapid commercialization combined with traditionalism in peasant societies causes peasants to revolt, the general statement would be limited to existing peasant societies with known combinations of causally relevant features. It is entirely possible that peasant societies with different configurations of causally relevant features may have existed in the past or may exist in the future (or were simply overlooked) and that these peasant societies experience revolts for entirely different reasons. Rapid commercialization and traditionalism might be irrelevant in these cases. This, of course, would not change the results of the analysis, but it is important to have some sense of the limitations on diversity.

Recall that one of the primary goals of the qualitative comparative approach is to allow maximum causal complexity—to avoid making simplifying assumptions about causes *at the outset,* as is done in most conventional statistical analyses. As I show below, simplifying assumptions might be considered later, but only after conducting an analysis allowing maximum complexity.

As an illustration of this problem consider the following simple truth table. An investigator believes that there are three causes relevant to the emergence of ethnic political parties in peripheral regions: ethnic inequality (A), centralization of government (B), and the erosion of ethnic institutions by national (that is, dominant culture) mass media (C). The truth table for several nations with ethnic minorities concentrated in peripheral regions is shown in Table 7.

Simple inspection indicates that condition C is the only cause of party formation (F) because there is a perfect correspondence between the presence/absence of erosion and the presence/absence of ethnic political parties, at least among existing causal combinations. But note that there are no cases combining erosion of ethnic institutions, ethnic inequality, and centralized government. It is quite possible that in the presence of both these conditions, the erosion of ethnic institutions might not prompt the formation of ethnic political parties. A *conservative* statement of what the truth table shows,

TABLE 7: Hypothetical Truth Table on Formation of Ethnic Political Parties

Condition			Party Formation	Cases
A	B	C	F	
0	0	0	0	5
0	0	1	1	3
0	1	0	0	7
0	1	1	1	8
1	0	0	0	9
1	0	1	1	4
1	1	0	?	0
1	1	1	?	0

A = Ethnic inequality
B = Centralized government
C = Erosion of ethnic institutions

therefore, is $F = aC + bC$, not $F = C$. In the first statement, C is necessary but not sufficient; in the second, C is both necessary and sufficient. Note that it is evident from the first equation what *simplifying* assumption is needed to produce the simpler causal statement ($F = C$): in the presence of both A and B, C causes F. This approach to diversity is quite different from making general assumptions about the operation of causes at the outset.

In most statistical analyses the problem of limited diversity is obscured because of the assumptions that are made about populations and samples, about variables and their relationships, and about the nature of causation (for example, that causes are additive; see Chapter 4). In qualitative comparative research these assumptions are avoided because cases are treated as interpretable combinations of characteristics, not as arrays of sample values.

It is possible to use a Boolean truth-table approach to address diversity. Causally relevant features of cases are used as input variables, following the pattern in the examples of Chapter 6, but the output variable is not an outcome or some type of historically emergent phenomenon. It is simply a presence/absence dichotomy indicating whether or not a certain combination of causes exists. The analysis thus focuses directly on the degree of diversity among cases. When all combinations of causal conditions exist (maximum diversity), the equation simplifies to unity (all combinations present; none absent). Applying these procedures to the simple truth table (Table 7) produces the following Boolean equation modeling diversity:

Existing combinations $= a + b$

This equation shows that all existing combinations display an absence of A or an absence of B (or, by logical implication, an absence of both A and B). Using De Morgan's Law (see Chapter 6) it is a simple matter to convert this into an explicit statement of the causal combinations that do not exist:

Nonexistent combinations $= AB$

Consider a more complex example. Table 8 presents hypothetical data on four causes of peasant revolts. Before attempting to assess the different combinations of conditions that cause revolts, it is possible, as a preliminary, to assess the diversity of causal combinations among peasant societies that

TABLE 8: Hypothetical Truth Table on Causes of Peasant Revolts
(Includes Contradictory Rows)

Conditions				Number of Instances	Output Code Presence/ Absence P	Output Code Revolt R
A	B	C	D			
0	0	0	0	4	1	0
0	0	0	1	10	1	0
0	0	1	0	0	0	?
0	0	1	1	5	1	1
0	1	0	0	4	1	0
0	1	0	1	2	1	0
0	1	1	0	0	0	?
0	1	1	1	4	1	1
1	0	0	0	10	1	0
1	0	0	1	0	0	?
1	0	1	0	2	1	0
1	0	1	1	0	0	?
1	1	0	0	0	0	?
1	1	0	1	5	1	1
1	1	1	0	0	0	?
1	1	1	1	9	1	1

A = Peasant traditionalism
B = Commercialization of agriculture
C = Middle peasants
D = Absentee landed elites

exist. This step is important because the results of any analysis of the causes of peasant revolts are limited to causal combinations exhibited by peasant societies actually included in the analysis.

In the truth table presented in Table 8, four conditions are examined: A indicates the persistence of peasant traditionalism (1 = yes, 0 = no); B indicates the commercialization of agriculture (1 = yes, 0 = no); C indicates the existence of a substantial class of middle peasants (1 = yes, 0 = no); and D indicates the residential preferences of the landed elite (1 = absentee, 0 = resident). Not all logically possible combinations of these four characteristics exist. Thus, the output variable P is coded 1 if there are instances of peasant societies with the combination of characteristics described in the row and coded 0 otherwise; the output variable R shows the subset of existing peasant societies with revolts.

In order to assess the limitations on the diversity among these cases, it is necessary simply to apply the minimization algorithms presented in Chapter 6 to this truth table, using P rather than R as the output value. An equation modeling existing combinations is derived; then De Morgan's Law is applied to this equation to create an explicit Boolean statement of the causal combinations that do not exist.

The first step of the Boolean analysis is to produce the prime implicants. Generally, the greater the variety of primitive expressions that enter into this part of Boolean minimization, the smaller the number of prime implicants. A small number of prime implicants indicates greater diversity because more combinations of conditions are covered.

There are many compatible rows in this truth table. The first two, for example, are compatible (they both produce P—that is, they exist—and differ on only one causal variable) and can be combined to form the expression abc. The specification of each step in the process of combining compatible rows would be tedious and therefore is not reported. This process of combining compatible rows, which involves only rows with 1's as output values, results in a partially reduced sums-of-products equation, which can be reduced further through the use of a prime implicant chart (see Chapter 6). The results of this further reduction are

$$P = ac + aD + BD + Abd$$

The equation shows that there are four basic types of peasant societies: those combining a low level of peasant traditionalism (a) and few middle peasants (c); those combining a low level of peasant traditionalism (a)

and absentee landlords (*D*); those combining commercialized agriculture (*B*) and absentee landlords (*D*); and those combining peasant traditionalism (*A*), little commercialization of agriculture (*b*), and resident landed elites (*d*). Referring to the truth table, we see that several examples of mixed types exist. Peasant societies conforming to combination *aBcD*, for example, have elements from the first three terms identified in the preceding equation.

De Morgan's Law can be used here to formulate an explicit statement of causal combinations that do not exist in the truth table:

$$p = ABd + aCd + AbD + BCd$$

This equation states the limits of any analysis of the truth table. Of course, this is all preliminary to an analysis of the causes of peasant revolts. These two equations (of the causal combinations that exist and those that do not) simply establish the substantive boundaries of the analysis of the causes of revolts.

Because instances of peasant revolt are a subset of instances of peasant societies, the equation for revolts is a subset of the equation for peasant societies. The simplest way to approach the causes of revolts is to assume that if any of the types of peasant societies that do not exist actually did exist, they would not experience revolts. (The fact that these combinations do not exist may indicate that they combine incompatible elements and therefore are unlikely ever to exist, much less experience revolts.) In this approach, combinations of causes that do not exist in the data should be coded as instances of nonrevolts. (Thus ? in the column for *R* in Table 8 is recoded to 0.) A reduction of this truth table shows (after producing prime implicants and applying the prime implicant chart procedure):

$$R = ABD + aCD$$

It is apparent from simple inspection that these two terms embrace a subset of the terms covered in the equation modeling causal combinations that exist. Specifically, the term *ABD* from the equation for *R* is a subset of the term *BD* from the equation for *P*, and the term *aCD* (*R* equation) is a subset of the term *aD* (*P* equation). (This is logically necessary because, as noted, instances of revolt form a subset of instances of relevant peasant societies.) Thus, peasant revolts are found only in two of the four basic types of peasant societies revealed in the Boolean analysis of diversity.

The preceding equation states that there are two major combinations of conditions that produce peasant revolts. The first type combines traditionalism (A), commercialization of agriculture (B), and absentee landlords (D). The second combines low traditionalism (a), middle peasants (C), and absentee landlords (D). The two types are best distinguished by the presence/absence of traditionalism and thus are mutually exclusive. One commonality, according to these results, is absentee landlords (D), which can be considered a necessary condition for revolts because it appears in both terms. In subsequent phases of research on peasant revolts, the investigator would use these two causal combinations to classify revolts and to interpret cases within each category.

While this might be an adequate stopping point for the Boolean analysis, it is possible to reduce the equation for revolts (R) further through simplifying assumptions. Recall that in the simple truth table on the formation of ethnic parties (Table 7) it was possible to simplify $F = aC + bC$ to $F = C$ by *assuming* that in the presence of AB (ethnic inequality and centralized government) C (erosion of ethnic institutions) would stimulate F. (There were no instances of ethnic inequality combined with centralized government.) Parallel assumptions can be made here in the analysis of peasant revolts to simplify further the equation $R = ABD + aCD$.

Here it is important to point out that this procedure involves selecting terms from the equation for combinations that do not exist (the equation for p) and adding these terms to the equation for R. Of course, only a subset of the terms covered by the equation for p are actually useful. Rather than go through the nonexistent combinations one by one to see if they might help, a simple shortcut algorithm can be used.

This shortcut has two steps. Both steps involve minor alterations of the procedures used to derive an equation for R. First, in the derivation of prime implicants, nonexistent combinations are treated as instances of the output variable (in this analysis, as instances of revolts). Second, when using the prime implicant chart to simplify the equation further, these terms (the nonexistent terms) are *excluded* from the primitive expressions that must be covered by the prime implicants. Essentially, these two alterations allow the derivation of simpler prime implicants without expanding the number of primitive expressions that must be covered in the prime implicant chart.

Applying these procedures to the truth table on peasant revolts (Table 8) results in the following reduced equation (with R primed to indicate that simplifying assumptions have been incorporated):

$$R' = AB + CD$$

It is clear that this is a superset of the previous equation ($R = ABD + aCD$) because the two terms have been expanded—the first to include in its coverage both $ABcd$ and $ABCd$ (that is, ABd) and the second to include in its coverage $AbCD$ ($ABCD$ was already covered by ABD). There are no instances of these three terms ($ABcd$, $ABCd$, and $AbCD$) in the original truth table. By assuming that if these causal combinations existed they would produce revolts, it was possible to reduce further the equation for R, modeled as R'.

This last equation states that peasant revolts are likely if peasant traditionalism (A) and commercialization of agriculture (B) are combined, or if a substantial class of middle peasants (C) is combined with absentee landlords (D). In order to produce a solution this minimal, it was necessary to assume (1) that in the presence of resident landlords (d) the combination of peasant traditionalism (A) and commercialized agriculture (B) would result in peasant revolts (R) and (2) that in the presence of peasant traditionalism (A) and little commercialization (b) the combination of middle peasants (C) and absentee landlords (D) would produce peasant revolts.

Essentially, these procedures formalize (and objectify) what many case-oriented researchers do in the course of their research. While the ideal social scientific comparison has the form of an experiment—only one causal condition at a time is allowed to vary—this rarely happens in practice. Almost all social scientific comparisons are incomplete—several causally relevant variables will differ across each pair of cases. When a comparativist cites these incomplete comparisons as evidence in support of a causal argument, assumptions are made concerning what would happen if various nonexistent combinations of causal conditions actually existed. Rarely are these assumptions made explicit, and as a consequence the charge is frequently made that comparativists let their interests (ideological and otherwise) impinge on their work. These interests, the charge continues, are hidden by comparativists in assumptions.

While there is certainly truth to the charge of hidden (and not so hidden) interests, it is usually difficult, if not impossible, for the comparativist to keep track of the many incomplete comparisons, and the implicit assumptions about nonexistent causal combinations these entail, when an investigation examines a variety of causal conditions in a range of cases. The Boolean approach to qualitative comparison not only makes it possible to keep track of the complexity of the comparisons but also requires objectification of assumptions about nonexistent causal combinations. In many respects these assumptions constitute an important part of the theory that a comparativist brings to an investigation. They are clear evidence of the use of theory to further causal generalization.

Of course, it is not necessary to make such assumptions, and both assumptions in the example involving peasant revolts could be questioned on theoretical and empirical grounds. The point is simply that the truth table approach makes explicit what is often implicit in other procedures. It allows direct consideration of combinations of causal conditions that do not exist in the data and thereby forces the investigator to confront the theoretical assumptions that permit more general causal statements.

It is important at this point to summarize at a more abstract level the logic of these procedures for addressing limited diversity. First, an equation describing configurations of causal conditions in existing cases was derived. The equation modeled diversity and was represented by the set P, indicating presence. De Morgan's Law was applied to this equation to produce an explicit statement (labeled p) describing nonexistent cases. Then an equation describing the combination of causes for the subset of P (peasant societies) experiencing revolt (R) was derived. Finally, an equation describing *possible* instances of peasant revolts (R') was derived by using a subset of the cases that do not exist (p) to simplify further the equation for revolts (R). Note that R is the intersection of P (combinations of causes that exist) and R' (possible combinations of causes of peasant revolts). Thus, R' can be seen as the model of peasant revolts that *might* be obtained if peasant societies were not limited in their diversity—that is, if peasant societies exhibiting all possible combinations of causes of peasant revolts could be examined.

Thus, Boolean techniques of qualitative comparative analysis provide a very direct approach to the problem of limited diversity. Limitations on diversity are modeled; implicit, simplifying assumptions are clarified and brought forward for examination; and an equation incorporating these assumptions can be derived if desired. In effect, the investigator is able to circumvent the problem of limited diversity in a way that objectifies the specific, empirical assumptions that allow the problem to be circumvented. The result is a model based on available evidence that, in effect, permits speculation about combinations of causes that do not exist.

Of course, these procedures are not mandatory. It is entirely possible that the more complex equation (the equation for R) might be preferred for several reasons. Certainly it is more conservative. Moreover, no simplifying assumptions about nonexistent combinations have been made. And, finally, maximum parsimony may not be desired, especially if the goal of interpretation, of appreciating and comprehending complexity, is given precedence over the goal of parsimony. Generally, when the number of relevant cases is relatively small, as in the present example, it is feasible to interpret individual cases or groups of similar cases. This situation favors using the more complex equation ($R = ABD + aCD$) over the equation incorporating simplifying assumptions ($R' = AB + CD$).

THE PROBLEM OF CONTRADICTIONS

In order to use the truth table approach presented above, it is necessary to determine an output value for each row (that is, a 1 or 0 for every combination of causes that exists in the data). So far, it has been assumed that this is not a problem. Empirical cases are only occasionally this neat, however, and it is necessary to consider what to do when the cases conforming to some of the combinations of causes do not exhibit clear tendencies toward presence or absence of the phenomenon of interest.

There are several ways to approach this problem. The best is to follow the lead of case-oriented researchers. Recall that when case-oriented researchers are confronted with inconsistencies or paradoxes comparable to contradictory rows, they typically examine the troublesome cases in greater detail and attempt to identify omitted causal variables (see Chapter 3). If five of the ten cases of *Abcd* in the hypothetical analysis of peasant revolts experienced revolts, for example, following the lead of case-oriented researchers would involve examining these ten cases in greater detail. This examination might lead to the conclusion that there is a fifth cause, E, that had been overlooked. If the addition of variable E divided the ten cases into groups more consistent with the revolt/nonrevolt distinction, then this fifth cause could be added to the truth table before reducing it. To follow the case-oriented approach, then, is to treat any specification of relevant causal conditions as tentative and to use theoretical and substantive knowledge to achieve a proper specification of causal conditions before reducing the truth table.

It is possible to use a truth table approach to aid the analysis of troublesome causal combinations and thereby simplify the task of identifying omitted causal variables. Essentially, an equation modeling contradictory causal

TABLE 9: Revised Truth Table on Peasant Revolts

Conditions				Number of Total Instances	Number of Instances of Revolt	Output Code Revolt R
A	B	C	D			
0	0	0	0	4	1	0
0	0	0	1	10	3	0
0	0	1	0	0	—	—
0	0	1	1	5	5	1
0	1	0	0	4	0	0
0	1	0	1	2	0	0
0	1	1	0	0	—	—
0	1	1	1	4	4	1
1	0	0	0	10	5	?
1	0	0	1	0	—	—
1	0	1	0	2	1	?
1	0	1	1	0	—	—
1	1	0	0	0	—	—
1	1	0	1	5	3	?
1	1	1	0	0	—	—
1	1	1	1	9	5	?

A = Peasant traditionalism
B = Commercialization of agriculture
C = Middle peasants
D = Absentee landed elites

combinations is derived. This equation is then used to guide the search for additional causal variables or to refine the existing analysis in some way. Consider the revised version of the truth table on peasant revolts (Table 8) presented in Table 9.

Note that four causal combinations (denoted with question marks) are split fairly evenly between revolts and no revolts. To analyze the commonalities shared by these four combinations, it is necessary simply to code them 1 and code other existing combinations 0. (Rows coded 0 or 1 on R in the truth table are recoded to 0 because they exhibit clear tendencies toward revolts or the absence of revolts.) The new output is labeled X and indicates contradictory causal combinations.

This new truth table can be reduced by using standard minimization procedures. The first step in the reduction treats nonexistent combinations (those coded "—" in the truth table) as though they were coded 0 (non-contradictory). The assumption is that if there were instances of these causal combinations, they could be coded 1 or 0 on R unambiguously. The results of this analysis are

$$X = ABD + Abd$$

The equation shows that when these two basic combinations of causes occur in peasant societies, revolts may or may not occur. In other combinations, revolts either tend to occur or tend not to occur.

This equation can be further reduced through simplifying assumptions. As in the analysis of R and R', it is possible to produce an equation for X'—an equation that models the causal combinations that might be contradictory if all logically possible combinations of causes existed. This procedure follows the outline given above: first, prime implicants are produced by using recoded nonexistent combinations (now coded 1); then, the prime implicant chart procedure is used, excluding the nonexistent combinations from the primitive terms that must be covered by the prime implicants. The results of this analysis show

$$X' = A$$

(Refer to Table 9 for verification.) Both the equation for X and the equation for X' are unambiguous in the guidance they give. The equation for X shows that contradictory causal combinations occur whenever A (peasant traditionalism) is combined with either BD or bd. The equation for X' shows that contradictory causal combinations occur whenever A (peasant traditionalism) is present.

This (hypothetical) result suggests two possible avenues for resolving the contradictions in the truth table. One is to attempt to clarify what is meant by peasant traditionalism. It may be that in some contexts peasant traditionalism is rigid adherence to an ancient and enduring way of life. In others, it may indicate a system of expectations and obligations linking peasant communities to landed elites and the state. In short, the results of this Boolean analysis might indicate problems in the conceptualization of traditionalism.

Alternatively, the results might indicate that the search for a fifth variable should focus on the (as yet unspecified) conditions that make peasant traditionalism revolutionary. It could be that peasant traditionalism has to be combined with conditions not included in the table (such as direct exposure of peasants to world market forces) for peasant traditionalism to take on a revolutionary cast.

The procedures outlined above for addressing ambiguous causal combinations are mainly oriented toward refining the investigator's concepts or understanding of cause. Thus, they force the investigator to return to the data and ultimately to construct a new truth table for the analysis of revolts. Sometimes it is difficult to return to the data, and alternative strategies, which do not follow the lead of the case-oriented approach, must be used. Several are addressed briefly here.

One simple solution is to code all ambiguous causal combinations 0. The argument here is that if no clear tendency (such as presence or absence of revolts) is apparent among the cases conforming to a certain causal combination, then the output should be coded conservatively (with respect to the investigator's confidence in the specification of conditions causing revolts). Thus, the analysis would show which causal combinations are unambiguously associated with the outcome (peasant revolts). Applying this rule to Table 9 results in the following reduced equation:

$$R = aCD$$

Essentially, this equation is a subset of the original equation for revolts, which showed $R = ABD + aCD$.

Alternatively, the investigator might want to recode contradictory combinations to nonexistent combinations, in which case the rows with "?" would be coded "—" to indicate that these combinations are being treated as though they do not exist. The effect of this procedure is to allow the algorithm to determine which final output value the contradictory rows should receive. If they help to produce a more minimal solution, they receive a coding of 1; if they do not, they receive a coding of 0. The results of this analysis also show that

$$R = aCD$$

A third alternative along these same lines would be to argue that a wide net should be cast so that all possible combinations of causes of peasant revolts are captured by the equation. This approach would be consistent with a general goal of allowing greater complexity. As noted in previous chapters, greater sensitivity to causal complexity is a hallmark of interpretive approaches. Thus, an equation that allows more causal combinations to be included among those thought to cause peasant revolts might be produced if ambiguous causal combinations are coded as 1 (revolts present) in the truth table. The results of this analysis reveal that

$$R = ABD + aCD + Abd$$

It is easy to see that this equation is a superset of the original equation for R. It adds causal combination Abd (peasant traditionalism combined with little commercialization and resident landlords). This is one of the causal combinations that originally appeared in the equation for C (contradictory causal combinations) above. Note that this equation answers the question: under what conditions are peasant revolts possible?

In general, it is better to resolve contradictions through examination of cases, the first strategy mentioned above, than to resolve them by assuming that contradictory rows are instances of the phenomenon of interest (1), instances of its absence (0), or nonexistent causal combinations (—).

The problem of contradictory causal combinations is not as serious as it might seem. In some investigations it is possible to incorporate frequency or statistical criteria to resolve contradictions. In general, if there are few cases there will be few contradictions. As the number of cases increases, so will the number of contradictions. But as the number of cases increases, it also becomes more feasible to apply simple statistical criteria to aid the construction of truth tables.

In some investigations every causal combination may be contradictory, and the investigator may be faced with an array of probabilities of success (that is, of positive outcome) for each causal combination. In order to recode these probabilities into positive (1) and negative (0) outcome combinations, it is possible to assess the significance of the difference between each probability and a substantively meaningful probability defined as a standard (for example, the probability of success in the entire set of cases considered as a single set). Causal combinations with probabilities significantly less than the standard could be coded as failures (0); causal combinations with probabilities significantly greater than the standard could be coded as successes (1); and causal combinations with probabilities not significantly different from the standard could be used selectively to produce a more minimal solution, as nonexistent combinations were used in the preceding example. (A variation of this procedure was used by Ragin and others 1984 in a study of discrimination.) Generally, these significance tests probably should use a high cutoff value (for example, significantly different at the 0.33 level) to minimize the number of causal combinations relegated to the third category (ambiguous outcome).

A second, more complex statistical procedure might be to use an additive, logit model of the outcome of interest to compute expected values for each combination of values on the independent variables. The deviations of the observed proportions from the expected values could then be used as a basis for coding the output value in the truth table. (Large positive deviations would be coded 1; large negative deviations would be coded 0.) Using these procedures would orient the analysis toward an exhaustive examination of *patterns* of statistical interaction using Boolean techniques. Of course, if there are very many cases it is also possible to conduct a Boolean analysis *and* a log-linear analysis (testing for complex statistical interactions) of the same data and use one to aid the interpretation of the other.

All solutions to the problem of contradictions, except the first, violate the spirit of case-oriented qualitative research and should be used only when it is impossible to return to the original cases and construct a better truth table. In many respects, once a truth table is completed (or at least treated as final), the investigation is oriented toward deciphering complexity as represented in the truth table. The lesson here is that an existing data set should not be considered an irrevocable starting point. In qualitative comparative work, the representation of the empirical world in terms of a truth table is a crucially important part of the investigation.

EVALUATING THEORETICAL ARGUMENTS

Theories do more than specify causal variables; they also specify causal combinations. A review of theoretical literature on peasant revolts, for example, could be used as a basis for specifying several causal conjunctures. One theory might argue that the simple commercialization of peasant societies is what stimulates revolts. Another might argue that peasant societies which are less traditional and have a large class of middle peasants living in communities with resident landed elites might be the most likely to revolt. These two theoretical arguments are easy to express in Boolean terms. The first (using the same notation as above) is simply $T = B$, where T indicates that the expectation is theoretically derived. The second is $T = aCd$. The two can be expressed in a single equation:

$$T = B + aCd$$

Obviously, this is not what the analysis of hypothetical data on peasant revolts showed. The less conservative equation (the one that incorporated simplifying assumptions about nonexistent combinations) from the analysis of peasant revolts revealed that

$$R' = AB + CD$$

(This simpler equation for revolts is used in the examples that follow to streamline the presentation.)

It is a simple matter to use Boolean algebra to map areas of agreement and disagreement between the theoretically derived model (T) and the results of the analysis of the truth table (R'). This analysis is important because it provides a basis for evaluating theory and interpreting empirical cases relative to theoretical expectations.

The intersection of T and R', for example, shows the subset of causal combinations that were both hypothesized and found:

$$
\begin{aligned}
(T)(R') &= (B + aCd)(AB + CD) \\
&= AB + BCD
\end{aligned}
$$

Essentially, this result shows that a subset of the causal conditions hypothesized by the first theory was confirmed. This theory predicted that all peasant societies experiencing commercialization should experience revolts. The results showed that only a subset of such societies actually experienced revolt.

It is also possible to use these procedures to model causal combinations that were found to produce revolts but were not hypothesized to do so by theory. This set is formed from the intersection of R' and t. Set t embraces all causal combinations not hypothesized to produce revolts and results from the application of De Morgan's Law to the equation for T:

$$
\begin{aligned}
t &= Ab + bc + bD \\
(t)(R') &= (Ab + bc + bD)(AB + CD) \\
&= AbCD + bCD \\
&= bCD
\end{aligned}
$$

The term bCD pinpoints the major shortcomings of existing theories. Specifically, the results show that these theories are off the mark when it comes to the causes of peasant revolts in the absence of commercialization (B). When commercialization is absent, revolts occur in peasant societies combining middle peasants and absentee landed elites.

This equation for $(t)(R')$ is important because it suggests a route for interpreting peasant revolts in peasant societies that are not experiencing commercialization. The equation states simply that in the absence of commercialization (a hypothesized cause), CD (the combination of middle peasants and resident landed elites) causes peasant revolts. In interpreting cases of

CD, an investigator might want to determine what it is about the *CD* combination that makes it causally equivalent to *B* (commercialization) or equivalent to the combination of commercialization and traditionalism (*AB*). This interpretive lead would be important if existing theory alone is used as a guide in interpreting peasant revolts.

Finally, it is also possible to model causal combinations that were hypothesized but not found to cause revolts. This set is formed from the intersection of *T* and *r'*. Set *r'* embraces all nonrevolts and can be derived by applying De Morgan's Law to *R'*:

$$r' = ac + ad + bc + bd$$
$$(T)(r') = (B + aCd)(ac + ad + bc + bd)$$
$$= aBc + aBd + aCd$$

These results show that the second theory, which emphasizes causal combination *aCd,* is not supported in any way by the evidence because the causal combination it proposes (*aCd*) appears in the preceding equation. The equation also shows that the first theory overstates the power of commercialization (*B*). When commercialization is combined with an absence of peasant traditionalism and either few middle peasants (*c*) or resident landed elites (*d*), revolts do not occur. This last equation shows the major shortcomings of existing theories; it refines the first theory and completely rejects the second.

These procedures show one of the decisive benefits of the Boolean approach to qualitative comparison. When theories are tested with traditional statistical techniques, investigators rarely are forced to consider causal conjunctures. These analytic techniques bias investigators toward viewing different causes as competitors in the struggle to explain variation. In the Boolean approach, by contrast, arguments about causal conjunctures are favored over arguments about single causes. Thus, investigators are forced to think in terms of conjunctures. At a minimum, the typical Boolean analysis forces an investigator who favors a single-variable explanation to consider the conjunctural limitations on its effects.

Generally, Boolean techniques should not be used mechanically; they are conceived as aids to interpretive analysis. The results of Boolean analysis do not take the place of interpretive analysis; the task of applying the results to cases remains once a solution has been obtained. Furthermore, it is important to emphasize that the construction of a truth table involves considerable effort—an intellectual labor that has been taken for granted in all these

examples. To construct a useful truth table, it is necesaary to gain familiarity with the relevant theories, the relevant research literature, and, most
important of all, the relevant cases. Thus, a truth table presupposes an enor-
mous amount of background research.

In all the examples presented above (and across the three issues examined—limited diversity, ambiguous causal combinations, and the evaluation
of theories), the general flexibility of the Boolean approach to qualitative
comparison was emphasized. Of course, it is much easier to demonstrate
this flexibility with actual data, the goal of Chapter 8, because data that are
not hypothetical are both more demanding and more interpretable. Before
presenting analyses of empirical data, however, I want to review the basic
characteristics of the Boolean approach and evaluate its potential as a basis
for a broadly comparative research strategy.

THE BOOLEAN APPROACH AS A MIDDLE ROAD

In Chapter 5, five ideal features of a synthetic comparative research strategy
were proposed. These included:

1. An ability to examine a large number of cases
2. An ability to address complex causal conjunctures
3. An ability to produce parsimonious explanations (if desired)
4. An ability to investigate cases both as wholes and as parts
5. An ability to evaluate competing explanations

Does the Boolean approach provide the necessary tools?

First, it is clear that the Boolean approach can handle many cases. In fact,
the actual number of cases is not a major consideration. If many cases have
the same combination of values on the causal variables of interest, they are
all coded together as a single row of the truth table because they are identical. The Boolean approach is more concerned with the different combinations of values that exist—and their output values—than with the actual
number of instances of each combination. More relevant than the number of
cases is the number of logically possible combinations of relevant causal conditions—a figure which is determined by the number of causal conditions
considered.

Second, it is clear that the Boolean approach addresses complex patterns
of interaction—patterns of multiple conjunctural causation. Essentially, the
Boolean approach begins by assuming maximum causal complexity, and
each combination of causal conditions is assigned its own output value. This

complexity is then simplified logically by using a few basic Boolean principles. This procedure contrasts sharply with the statistical approach which begins by assuming simplicity.

Note that the Boolean approach accomplishes what case-oriented investigators attempt, but on a much larger scale. In case-oriented studies, investigators analyze similarities and differences in order to identify common underlying patterns and types. As noted in Chapter 3, however, the web of similarities and differences frequently gets out of hand. The Boolean truth-table approach and its rules for simplifying complexity provide a basis for managing this complicated web. It allows case-oriented investigators to see and comprehend complex patterns and conjunctures.

Third, the Boolean approach, through its minimization procedures, is capable of producing parsimonious explanations. The problem of parsimony is fundamentally a question of theoretically guided data reduction. All data reduction techniques produce parsimony. The construction of a raw data matrix is a form of parsimony—as is the construction of a truth table from a raw data matrix—because complexity has been greatly reduced. It has been captured and transformed into coded variables. A parsimonious *explanation* goes beyond these simple data reductions by linking causes and effects in a theoretically based and meaningful (that is, interpretable) manner. This further reduction of complexity is accomplished in statistical analyses in the estimation of the unique additive contribution of each independent variable to some outcome variable. In the Boolean approach a parsimonious explanation is achieved by determining the largest classes of conditions for which a certain outcome is obtained. Simply stated, applications of Boolean techniques of data reduction culminate in logically minimal statements of the different combinations of conditions that produce certain outcomes.

Fourth, the Boolean approach is both holistic and analytic; it examines cases as wholes and as parts. In a Boolean analysis cases are seen as combinations of parts. These combinations can be interpreted as different situations. A fundamental principle of holism provides the metatheoretical basis for this way of seeing cases: to alter any single part of a whole, any element, is—potentially at least—to alter the character of the whole. This approach contrasts directly with most statistical approaches where the goal is to estimate the average effect of each variable (the causal importance of each part) across all values of other variables.

Yet the Boolean approach is not extreme in its holism. In its most extreme form, a holistic philosophy argues that each entity is unique, that cases cannot be compared with each other once they are understood in all their complexity and individuality. Obviously, the Boolean approach does not go this far. Cases with identical combinations of values on relevant causal variables are pooled in the construction of the truth table. For the purpose of Boolean analysis, they are equivalent wholes. Furthermore, the boundaries of uniqueness, of variation, are set by the causal conditions selected for examination. This constraint restricts the individuality that cases may display. If there are four causal conditions selected for analysis, for example, there are only sixteen possible wholes. In short, the Boolean approach is analytic in its approach to cases because it examines the same causal conditions in each setting. However, it is holistic in the way it compares different situations and in this manner preserves one of the best features of the case-oriented approach.

Fifth, and finally, the Boolean approach can be used to evaluate different explanations. One shortcoming of case-oriented studies is the fact that they are usually organized around a single perspective. Often, cases are used selectively to illustrate or elaborate a certain theory. In the Boolean approach, competing explanations can be operationalized in causal variables in a manner that is similar to statistical approaches. In statistical analyses, however, variables compete with each other. If one set of variables wins, then the theory they represent is supported. In the Boolean approach this competition between theories is transcended. Different combinations of causal conditions define different situations. In some situations the variables associated with a certain theory may be important. In others they may not. This feature provides a basis for evaluating competing explanations and for advancing theory. The typical end product of a Boolean analysis is a statement of the limits of the causal variables identified with different theories, not their mechanical rejection or acceptance.

A NOTE ON IMPLEMENTING BOOLEAN ALGORITHMS

While it is possible to use the simple pencil and paper techniques outlined above to address relatively small problems, it is far easier to use a computer to implement these algorithms. An experienced programmer can implement them on a microcomputer, for example, in BASIC. McDermott (1985: 401–415) lists a BASIC program implemented on a TRS-80 microcomputer that will minimize Boolean truth tables. Several minimal modifications of this program are necessary before it can be run on an MS-DOS computer (for example, an IBM-PC): first, replace the variables in the DIM statements with actual numbers, assuming a moderate number of inputs; second, delete the DATA statements (lines 18000–20170) and replace them with a front-end procedure to read a truth table from a file, using INPUT (to supply the name of the file containing the truth table), CLOSE, and OPEN statements; third, delete the statements beginning with CMD, substituting a GOTO 20 for the CMD statement in line 920; and, fourth, change the bracket character in the program listing ([) to BASIC's exponentiation character. The program will keep looping to request a file name with a truth table. Pressing the enter or the break key instead of naming a file will allow an exit from the program. The major drawback in applying McDermott's program to social data is that a clean and more or less fully specified truth table must be input into the program. Also, the program is not completely trouble free in the implementation just described, but for do-it-yourself types it is a good place to start.

Drass and Ragin (1986) have implemented Boolean algorithms in a microcomputer package called QCA (Qualitative Comparative Analysis) designed specifically for social data. It has a lot of bells and whistles compared to McDermott's program and allows greater flexibility in the handling of social data. Further, it expects a data matrix as input, not a clean and fully specified truth table.

8

Applications of Boolean Methods
of Qualitative Comparison

Boolean methods of qualitative comparison have a variety of research applications. The major emphasis of this book, of course, is their use in comparative social science. The principles of qualitative and holistic comparison
these techniques embody, however, are relevant to a variety of research
questions. Three representative applications are presented in this chapter.
The examples, of necessity, are brief. The intent is simply to convey the general flavor of Boolean-based qualitative analysis in a range of research areas.
All the examples involve use of relatively straightforward categorical data.
As noted previously, the principles of qualitative, holistic comparison are
much easier to implement and to grasp when applied to categorical data.

The three applications are presented in macro to micro order, beginning
with a reanalysis of some of Stein Rokkan's data on nation building in Western Europe and concluding with an analysis of data on organizations (juvenile courts in the United States). An application to individual-level data is
presented in Ragin and others (1984), which addresses the use of Boolean
methods to analyze data on discrimination. Finally, a truly microsociological
application—to typifying processes in the production of official records in
the criminal justice system—is presented by Drass and Spencer (1986).

The first application presented here is a reanalysis of data used by Rokkan
(1970) in his work on nation building in Western Europe. Rokkan used a
"configurational" approach that bears many similarities to the Boolean approach presented in this work. His main substantive interest was the growth
of mass democracy and the emergence of different cleavage structures in

Western European polities. One outcome that interested him was the division of *some* working-class movements in these countries following the Russian Revolution into internationally oriented wings and some into nationally oriented wings. He considered the distribution of this outcome important because of its implication for the future of working-class mobilization (and cleavage structures in general) in Western Europe.

The second application addresses the use of Boolean techniques in the study of comparative ethnic political mobilization. Three theories are used to guide the analysis of data on the causes of ethnic mobilization among territorially based linguistic minorities in Western Europe: the developmental perspective, the reactive ethnicity perspective, and the ethnic competition perspective. This application of Boolean techniques emphasizes their use to examine multiple conjunctural causation, to evaluate theories, and to lay a foundation for historical examination of specific cases or categories of cases.

The third application addresses organizations. It is an analysis of organizational characteristics of juvenile courts in the United States. The goal of this analysis is not to examine a causal outcome, per se, but to examine limitations on the diversity of organizational forms that exist among juvenile courts. In addition to showing how Boolean techniques can be used to construct empirical typologies, this example also shows how frequency criteria can be incorporated to produce both fine- and coarse-grained analyses.

APPLICATION TO NATION BUILDING: A REANALYSIS OF ROKKAN (1970)

Many of the methodological sentiments expressed in this study echo those voiced by Stein Rokkan in his pioneering work on nation building published in the late 1960s and early 1970s. Rokkan was disturbed by the gulf between case-oriented and variable-oriented study and proposed an explicitly configurational approach to comparative social research as a way to bridge the two strategies. The research strategy he outlined resembles the Boolean approach presented in this book in its emphasis on combinations of characteristics and holistic comparison of cases.

In a typical application of his configurational approach, Rokkan would establish three or four theoretically important dichotomies and then elaborate their different logically possible combinations. Countries manifesting each combination of values would then be selected, compared, and interpreted. These results, in turn, would be used as a basis for evaluating the heuristic value of the conceptual framework represented in the dichotomies. If the empirical examples of the different combinations of characteristics differed in predicted ways from each other, this was taken as evidence in favor of the value of the scheme as a guide to historical interpetation.

One of the issues that especially interested Rokkan was the timing and speed of the extension of the franchise in Western European countries and, by implication, the amount of conflict associated with the growth of mass democracy in each country. Three historical conditions defining different starting points in this process, he argued, shaped the progress of democratization: "medieval consolidation"—whether the country was a separate dynasty or a collection of cities and provinces within successive continental empires; "continuity of representative organs"—whether or not the country experienced extensive periods of absolutist rule; and "status in the international system"—whether a country was, or was part of, a *major* power or a *lesser* power. After examining the extension of the franchise in cases representative of each combination of values (there were only a few combinations lacking empirical instances), Rokkan concluded that the character of franchise extension was indeed shaped by different combinations of these three historical conditions—by the different starting points.

Often, Rokkan's configurational approach had a somewhat nebulous quality to it. In the example cited above, the dependent variable was the *character* of the growth of mass democracy. Thus, the analysis examined different historical conditions shaping the *nature* of this growth, not any particular feature of it. This aspect of Rokkan's work tilts it in a holistic, case-oriented direction—despite the generalizing, variable-oriented character that follows from applying the same framework to a range of cases.

Occasionally, however, Rokkan did address specific historical outcomes. One feature of the history of Western European polities that interested him, for example, was the variation among them in the impact of the Russian Revolution on working-class organizations. In some countries it had little impact, but in others it created deep and lasting divisions. A cursory examination of the cross-national distribution of these divisions does not yield simple conclusions. For example, Sweden and Norway are neighboring countries and share many features. Yet the success of the Russian Revolution, according to Rokkan, created only minor divisions in Swedish working-class organizations but major divisions in Norwegian organizations. True to form, Rokkan addressed this variation configurationally. In essence, he argued that the origins and nature of a polity's existing cleavage structure shaped the reaction of a country's working-class movement to the Russian Revolution.

It would be difficult, of course, to reproduce his entire argument on cleavage structures in this brief treatment. His main concern was the interests and alliances of the state-builders and how these factors shaped the nature of the opposition to the state-builders. Of necessity, these interests and alliances were historically grounded. Rokkan argued that the important historical factors shaping cleavage structures in Western European polities and their reactions to the Russian Revolution were the outcome of the Reformation, the outcome of the "Democratic Revolution" (1970:116), the outcome of the Industrial Revolution, and the timing of state formation. The important dichotomies related to these four factors were:

1.   Whether the state established a national church or remained allied with the Roman Catholic church. Rokkan labels this outcome "C" for national church.

2.   Whether or not the state allowed Roman Catholic participation in nation-building institutions, especially mass education. In countries with national churches, this indicates deep religious division. In countries that remained allied with the Roman Catholic church, this represents a failure to establish a more secular state. Obviously, this dichotomy is relevant only to countries with large numbers of Roman Catholics. Rokkan labels this outcome "R" for Roman Catholic.

3.   Whether the state maintained an alliance with landed interests or favored commercial and industrial interests over landed interests from the outset. Rokkan labels this outcome "L" for landed interests.

4.   Whether a state formed early (such as Spain) or late (such as Belgium). Rokkan labels this outcome "E" for early.

These four dichotomies yield sixteen different combinations of conditions. Rokkan identified empirical instances of ten of these combinations. (See Table 10.) The outcome variable in Table 10 is labeled "S" and indicates working-class parties that were split in their reaction to the Russian Revolution. (The codings presented in the table faithfully reproduce those supplied by Rokkan. The goal of this discussion is to present a methodology suitable for configurational comparisons, not to challenge Rokkan's substantive interpretations of specific cases.)

After examining the different combinations of conditions and their associated outcomes, Rokkan (1970:132–138) concludes that in Protestant countries (that is, those with national churches) the working-class movement tended to be much more divided if the nation-building process was

TABLE 10: Rokkan's Data on Divided Working-Class Movements in Western Europe

Country	C	R	L	E	S
Great Britain	1	0	1	1	0
Denmark	1	0	0	1	0
Sweden	1	0	0	1	0
Norway	1	0	0	0	1
Finland	1	0	0	0	1
Iceland	1	0	0	0	1
Germany	1	1	1	0	1
Netherlands	1	1	0	1	0
Switzerland	1	1	0	1	0
Spain	0	0	1	1	1
France	0	0	0	1	1
Italy	0	0	0	0	1
Austria	0	1	1	0	0
Ireland	0	1	1	0	0
Belgium	0	1	0	0	0
Luxembourg	0	1	0	0	0
No Instance	0	0	1	0	?
No Instance	0	1	0	1	?
No Instance	0	1	1	1	?
No Instance	1	0	1	0	?
No Instance	1	1	0	0	?
No Instance	1	1	1	1	?

C = National church (vs. state allied to Roman Catholic church)
R = Significant Roman Catholic population and Roman Catholic participation in mass education
L = State protection of landed interests
E = Early state
S = Major split in working-class movement provoked by Russian Revolution (outcome variable)

NOTE: Question marks indicate that no clear prediction is made.

more recent and, by implication, national identity less settled. In Catholic countries, by contrast, the deeper and more persistent the church–state conflict, the greater the division in the working-class movement. In general, it appears from these two combinations that the *less settled* polities (Protestant ones because of recency; Catholic ones because of continuing religious conflict) were the ones that experienced divided working-class movements.

It is easy to express Rokkan's conclusion in Boolean terms (with uppercase letters indicating presence and lowercase letters indicating absence), and it is roughly confirmed through simple inspection of the empirical data presented in truth table form in Table 10.

$$S = Ce + cr$$

The equation states simply that the Russian Revolution divided working-class movements (1) in countries with national churches that had experienced nation building more recently (Norway, Finland, Iceland, Germany) and (2) in countries without national churches (that is, Catholic countries) that had denied the Roman Catholic church a major role in mass education (Spain, France, Italy).

Rokkan's results are duplicated when the Boolean algorithms described in Chapters 6 and 7 are applied to these data, but *only if* the combinations of conditions without empirical instances (the last six rows in Table 10) are allowed to take on *any* output value. In this type of analysis, the algorithm may assign these rows 1's or 0's, whichever assignment produces the most logically minimal solution possible. As noted in Chapter 7, this is equivalent to incorporating simplifying assumptions that, in effect, make allowances for the limited diversity of social phenomena (in this case, the limited diversity of Western European countries).

Boolean analysis of Rokkan's data without these simplifying assumptions does *not* reproduce his results. The most conservative way to approach the data in the truth table is to assume that the six combinations of characteristics for which there are no empirical instances would not have divided working-class movements. This strategy is conservative only in the sense that it treats the division of the working class as an unusual phenomenon and, by implication, considers no division following the Russian Revolution (a likely consequence of sheer inertia) the normal state of affairs. This assumption is operationalized simply by coding the output for these six combinations of values to zero in Table 10.

Applying the Boolean minimization algorithms to the resulting truth table yields the following reduced expression:

$$S = rle + crE + CRLe$$

This equation is considerably more complex than the one allowing simplifying assumptions (that is, Rokkan's). It describes three different (mutually exclusive) combinations of conditions leading to divided working-class movements: (1) low Roman Catholic involvement in mass education in a more recently formed state that favored urban interests from the outset: Italy, Norway, Finland, and Iceland; (2) low Roman Catholic involvement in mass education in a Catholic country with a long history of state building: Spain and France; and (3) Roman Catholic involvement in mass education in a Protestant country with a recent history of state building allied with landed interests: Germany.

The two conditions identified by Rokkan (Ce and cr) are clearly visible in the last two terms of the second equation. Thus, the second and third terms in this equation could be considered elaborations of his basic argument which emphasized recency in Protestant countries and religiously based conflict in Catholic countries. Note, however, that the last term (the one relevant to his Ce combination) also includes religious conflict—Catholic involvement in mass education in a Protestant country. Thus, these elaborations of Rokkan's simpler terms give greater weight to a history of religious conflict. In many respects, therefore, both of these terms describe national situations where the pressure or weight of historically rooted conditions on political institutions and arrangements was great. (In many respects, the weight of history was comparably great in Russia.)

Considering these two terms alone, there is some resonance of the results with arguments made by Mann (1973) and echoed by Giddens (1973). Mann and Giddens present elaborate historical arguments concerning conditions that prompt the development of revolutionary working-class consciousness. They both argue that where the confrontation between a feudal past and modern institutions was most sudden and acute, revolutionary consciousness was most likely. To the extent that a divided working-class movement signals a greater reservoir of potential revolutionary consciousness, this argument is loosely supported by the last two terms in the equation.

The first term in the equation, however, is not consistent with Rokkan's argument or with the argument concerning the weight of historical cleavages developed above. The image conveyed by this combination is of a highly secular state (whether it is Protestant or Catholic is irrelevant) that is *relatively* free from historical constraints: it is not allied with landed interests, nor is it encumbered by historically rooted political institutions. This combination of conditions casts a very different light on the question of reactions to the Russian Revolution. It suggests that the Russian Revolution had a strong impact on polities (and working-class movements) that were less constrained by historical cleavages and more open to change. In short, the inertia of the past was easier to overcome in these cases.

Together, the three terms in the equation suggest that divided working-class movements were found in countries where the burden of historically rooted conditions on the polity was either relatively light or very heavy. This conclusion is qualitatively different from Rokkan's, which emphasized the degree to which different polities were "settled." Of course, this generalization is limited to Western Europe after the Russian Revolution. It would be hazardous to extend this statement beyond this region and period.

There is still another way to evaluate Rokkan's analysis. I noted above that if the six combinations lacking empirical instances are allowed to take on any output value, then it is possible to reproduce Rokkan's conclusion ($S = cr + Ce$) with Boolean techniques. However, this simpler solution requires simplifying assumptions. The important question to answer from this perspective is "what was Rokkan required to assume in order to produce this tidy solution?" This can be ascertained by contrasting the first solution, which incorporates simplifying assumptions, with the second, which does not.

An analysis of these differences shows that Rokkan assumed—implicitly—that countries with the following combinations of conditions, if they had existed, would have experienced divided working-class movements following the Russian Revolution: $CRle, rLe$. The first term describes a more recently formed Protestant nation-state with heavy Roman Catholic involvement in mass education and a bias toward urban interests. The second describes a recently formed nation-state with a bias toward landed interests and with low Catholic involvement in mass education. Of course, there are no clear instances of these two combinations within Western Europe, and Rokkan did not intend his argument to be applied outside this region. However, there are countries that roughly approximate these combinations outside of Western Europe, and these cases could be examined to see if they are consistent with Rokkan's expectations. This examination would provide an avenue for establishing a crude check on Rokkan's simplifying assumptions. The important point is not that these cases were not checked but that simplifying assumptions were implicitly incorporated. Boolean techniques provide a direct avenue for uncovering simplifying assumptions, which makes it possible to bring them forward for examination.

The intent of this application has not been to criticize Rokkan but simply to show how Boolean methods elaborate his configurational approach. Rokkan indicated that his conclusions were tentative. The ones offered here based on his classifications are even more tentative than Rokkan's. Rokkan's primary goal was to establish a foundation for examining the development and structure of cleavage systems in Western Europe. If anything, the reanalysis offered here simply confirms that the scheme he developed is useful, perhaps in ways he did not intend. Nevertheless, the goal of the re-analysis is compatible with Rokkan's—to provide a foundation for *understanding* historical patterns and political developments in Western European polities, not to *test* theory per se.

The next application of Boolean methods of comparison examines several perspectives and many more cases. It provides an opportunity to demonstrate in more detail the interplay between theory, qualitative comparative analysis, and historical investigation.

APPLICATION TO THE COMPARATIVE STUDY OF SUBNATIONS

From a nation-building perspective, the map of Western Europe is cluttered with territorially based ethnic minorities or "subnations" (Petersen 1975 : 182). At the periphery of most countries are linguistically distinct populations that differ substantially from the dominant or core cultural groups. France has Alsatians, Bretons, and Corsicans, among others; Great Britain has a variety of Celtic-speaking populations residing in its peripheral areas. Some countries are collections of subnations, and dominance is hotly contested. No Western European country is free from linguistically based ethnic diversity.

The political mobilization of territorially based linguistic minorities in industrialized countries is anomalous from the viewpoint of classic social theory. The dominant theme of this body of thought is developmental. According to this reasoning, economic and political forces associated with Western capitalism erode local cultures and gradually erase intranational cultural differences. Ethnic and cultural differences decline in importance as a basis for social action, and the possibility of ethnic political mobilization decreases. The experience of the last several decades, especially the late 1960s and early 1970s, however, contradicts these expectations. In all corners of Western Europe, and the world, there was a resurgence of ethnic political mobilization. The idea that the countries of Western Europe are integrated, modern polities free from serious ethnically or culturally based opposition has been discarded.

This section examines the conditions of ethnic political mobilization among territorially based linguistic minorities in Western Europe and attempts to shed some light on the diversity of subnations. Its primary goal is to illustrate the Boolean algorithms outlined in Chapters 6 and 7 with typical, if imperfect, comparative data. The outcome variable in these analyses is ethnic political mobilization. The causal variables describe different aspects of subnations relevant to such mobilization. These analyses are introduced with a discussion of current theories and research strategies in the study of ethnic political mobilization. I hope to show that the Boolean approach is particularly well suited for the analysis of comparative ethnic political mobilization because it is capable of comprehending the diversity of subnational situations.

THEORIES OF ETHNIC POLITICAL MOBILIZATION.   Contemporary theories of ethnic political mobilization do not allow conceptualization of the diversity of subnations. Each of the major perspectives—the developmental perspective, the reactive ethnicity perspective, and the ethnic competition perspective—either focuses on a single subnational situation or simply assumes intranational ethnic variation and emphasizes the general conditions that prompt ethnic political mobilization.

In the developmental perspective, ethnicity is viewed as a primordial sentiment (Geertz 1963) destined to wither away in societies that experience significant social structural differentiation (Parsons 1975). In a modern setting, therefore, ethnic mobilization is viewed as aberrant. It is possible only if there has been some failure to draw subnations into national economic life. This view of ethnic mobilization has been applied to the analysis of political cleavages in Western European countries by Lipset and Rokkan (1967 : 1–64). They argue that in Western European polities, culturally based political cleavages were superseded by functional cleavages reflecting economic interests.

In this perspective, the classic subnation is a culturally distinct, geographically peripheral collectivity that has remained relatively isolated economically and socially from the national center. The subnation may inhabit a resource-poor region of the nation, and its members may tend to specialize in primary economic activities such as farming. Ethnic political mobilization occurs because of the growing economic, cultural, and political divergence of the subnation from the rest of the nation. Ethnic mobilization resulting from regional economic inequality is not incompatible with this divergence, but the underlying basis for mobilization according to developmental logic is the failure to integrate the subnation, not its relative poverty per se. Rokkan

(1970 : 121), for example, argues that three conditions are responsible for the emergence and consolidation of territorial countercultures: territorial concentration (a condition common to all subnations examined here); social isolation (usually linked to the existence of strong linguistic differences); and economic isolation (especially, weak economic ties to the national core).

The second view, the reactive ethnicity perspective, argues that a particularistic allocation of valued roles and resources to the dominant ethnic group is the primary cause of ethnic political mobilization. In contrast to the developmental perspective, which argues that a particularistic allocation of scarce goods is incompatible with structural differentiation, the reactive ethnicity perspective argues that it can occur in societies at any level of structural differentiation. Thus, ethnic identity is preserved in modern societies by a coincidence of ethnicity and social class (Gellner 1969). This "cultural division of labor," Hechter (1975) argues, can exist even in an advanced industrial society. He asserts that urbanization and industrialization intensify the link between social class and ethnicity by concentrating members of subnations in low-status positions and neighborhoods (1975 : 39–43). Class mobilization, of course, exists as an alternative to ethnic mobilization in such societies, and, in fact, it may precede ethnic mobilization. However, should national working-class organizations fail to meet the demands of the culturally subordinate lower strata, ethnic political mobilization is likely (1975 : 309).

In common with the developmental perspective, the reactive ethnicity perspective sees the classic subnation as a relatively disadvantaged cultural minority residing in the periphery of an advanced nation-state. However, in this perspective the subnational area is not isolated; it has been infiltrated by members of the dominant cultural group. Typically, the members of the dominant collectivity see themselves as developers bearing the fruits of modern society. The development they bring to the subnational area is often stunted and distorted, however, because the region is developed as an appendage of the national economy. Its interests are subordinated to national interests, and capital may be drained from the subnation. Furthermore, peripheral social structure is distorted by the cultural division of labor that is instituted. The dominant strata come to be seen as alien by the lower strata, and the culture of the lower strata becomes stereotyped as inferior by members of the dominant strata. The peripheral region may be industrial, but typically it is poorer than the core region.

The ethnic competition perspective, the third major view, argues that social structural modernization affects nations and subnations in two ways.

First, modernization reduces ethnic diversity within subnations and within the dominant culture by eroding small-scale, local cultural identities. Second, modernization increases the importance of large-scale ethnic identities by altering the conditions of competition between politically definable collectivities (Hannan 1979). Specifically, because the size of the most powerful competitor (the core in a modern nation-state and the associated dominant cultural group) increases with modernization, organized resistance to the core succeeds only when it is organized around large-scale identities. Thus, modernization actually increases the political viability of broadly defined ethnic identities (Nielsen 1985). Ethnic political mobilization is sparked when ethnic groups (dominant and subordinate) are forced to compete with each other for the same rewards and resources. A competitive situation is especially likely when a stable cultural division of labor is disrupted by economic change (Ragin 1977, 1979; Nielsen 1980).

In the ethnic competition perspective, the classic subnation may or may not be peripheral. The primary requirement is one of size—it must be big enough in potential membership to muster a significant challenge to the core. In general, this perspective follows the lead of the resource mobilization perspective (Tilly 1978; McCarthy and Zald 1977; see Jenkins 1983, Nagel and Olzak 1982, Olzak 1983) in arguing that anything which adds to the resources of the subnation enhances its ability to challenge the core. According to this reasoning, rich subnations are more likely to mobilize successfully than poor subnations. A second major requirement is for some form of structurally based provocation. Many different contexts might provide a basis for this. Typically, however, this provocation involves a change in the structure of rewards and resources available to ethnic collectivities that intensifies the competition between them.

TESTING THEORIES OF ETHNIC POLITICAL MOBILIZATION. These three theories have been set against each other in several studies, and a more or less standard approach to testing them has emerged. (Recent investigations include Hechter 1975; Ragin 1977, 1979, 1986; Ragin and Davies 1981; Nielsen 1980; Olzak 1982; see also Nagel and Olzak 1986.) These studies typically examine cross-sectional and longitudinal data on the aggregate political tendencies of territorial units within single countries (such as vote percentages for different political parties in electoral districts in Belgium). This strategy is comparable to Shorter and Tilly's use of France to test general arguments about the political mobilization of workers in advanced countries. This general strategy has been strongly criticized by Lieberson (1985) and others.

Existing studies of ethnic mobilization pinpoint kinds of areas supportive of ethnic parties and shifts in these patterns over time. Different theories of ethnic political mobilization provide researchers with different images of subnations and different images of ethnic political mobilization. The images provided by these theories, in turn, are used to aid the formulation of hypotheses about aggregate patterns of support for ethnic parties, and quantitative data are used to test the hypotheses. Thus, only the implications of theories for patterns of support in different countries, considered one at a time, are examined. The theories have not been used to examine differences among a large number of instances of ethnic political mobilization across several countries. This limitation is important because the theories emphasize polity-level phenomena. The disruption of a stable cultural division of labor, for example, tends to be polity-wide.

While these studies have enriched social scientists' understanding of ethnic political mobilization, several basic questions remain unanswered. Many different subnations in Western Europe mobilized during the 1960s and 1970s, and there are striking differences among them. Did the same causal conditions prompt ethnic mobilization in each case? Are there underlying patterns or types? There is little reason to expect all instances of ethnic political mobilization to be alike. Further, not all subnations mobilized. No one has examined the subnations that failed to mobilize. The Boolean analysis presented here examines these questions. As I hope to show, it is useful for this kind of investigation because it allows conceptualization of the diversity of subnations.

A BOOLEAN APPROACH TO ETHNIC MOBILIZATION.   The first step in a Boolean analysis is to identify the relevant causal conditions. Using the three perspectives outlined above as guides, we can identify four major characteristics of subnations: the subnation's size, the strength of its linguistic base, its relative wealth, and its economic status (declining versus expanding). The outcome variable is ethnic political mobilization as indicated by a variety of achievements: formation of an ethnic political party, substantial membership in ethnic organizations, representation in national or regional legislative bodies, ethnic demonstrations and political violence, and so on. The data used to code these variables are based on reports by Allardt (1979), Kidron and Segal (1981), and McHale and Skowronski (1983).

The size of subnations is relevant primarily to the ethnic competition perspective. This perspective argues that challenges to the core cultural group must be based on the mobilization of broad minority identities embracing many members. While only the competition perspective emphasizes this factor, the other perspectives would not deny that size makes a difference. Thus, this variable does not sharply distinguish the three perspectives.

Good data on the size of ethnic groups are notoriously hard to obtain because they tend to be politically sensitive and because self-assignment to ethnic groups tends to be somewhat variable. It is possible to distinguish smaller and larger subnations in Western Europe, however, using 100,000 members as a cutoff value. This value was selected for two reasons: most subnations are clearly smaller or clearly larger than 100,000; moreover, the cutoff value is consistent with the goal of distinguishing collectivities capable of mounting a serious challenge. In the analysis that follows, subnations estimated to have fewer than 100,000 members were coded as small (0) and subnations estimated to have more than 100,000 members were coded as large (1).

The strength of the linguistic base is most relevant to the developmental perspective. This perspective argues that the persistence of minority culture is what causes ethnic political mobilization. This variable is also relevant to the ethnic competition perspective because a strong minority linguistic base is a resource that both enhances mobilization and intensifies ethnic competition. In the reactive ethnicity perspective, however, the expectation is that the dominant cultural group has launched an assault on the subnation's language and culture. Thus, a politically mobilized subnation may not have a strong linguistic base according to this perspective.

In the following analysis only subnations in which it is clear that the minority language is known to the vast majority of minority members (in both oral and written form) are coded as having a strong linguistic base (1). If the language is unknown to at least a substantial minority, it is coded as having a weak linguistic base (0). This strict coding is consistent with the emphases of all three theories.

Relative wealth of the subnation is most relevant to the reactive ethnicity perspective. This theory sees ethnic mobilization as a reaction to inequality and exploitation. The perception of exploitation is more likely if the subnation is poorer than core areas of the nation. A lower relative wealth could also, however, indicate divergence resulting from economic isolation, a major concern of the developmental perspective. Thus, relative wealth is also a concern of the developmental perspective. Finally, the ethnic competition perspective sees wealth as a resource and would argue that subnations with *greater* relative wealth are more likely to mobilize. Thus, this variable clearly distinguishes the ethnic competition perspective from the other two perspectives.

Data on regional differences in production per capita are used to assess relative wealth. If a subnation's gross production per capita is substantially less than that of the remainder of the nation, relative wealth is coded 0. Relative wealth is coded 1 if it is equal to or greater than that of the rest of the nation.

Economic status is relevant to all three perspectives. In the developmental perspective, the typical subnation is an isolated, declining region. This description is consistent with the idea that it is a backwater area. In the reactive ethnicity perspective, however, mobilization is stimulated by exploitation. Either decline or advance might signal more exploitation. Decline may indicate an accumulation of misery; advance may indicate that the dominant group has found new ways to exploit the subnation's resources, which, in turn, might further peripheralize it. Thus, the specific predictions of this perspective are unclear. Similarly, the ethnic competition perspective argues that any economic change (advance or decline) that alters the structure of rewards and resources is likely to provoke ethnic mobilization. This is because such changes are likely to stimulate ethnic competition.

Data on immigration are used to assess economic status. If immigration into a subnation exceeds emigration from a subnation, it is coded 1 (advancing) on economic status. If emigration exceeds or equals immigration, it is coded 0 (declining). Note that if immigration is greater than emigration, then economic ties linking the subnation to the national center are probably increasing in strength.

The three theoretical perspectives are compared with respect to their predictions concerning the four causal variables in Table 11. As noted, the perspectives do not contradict each other absolutely. There are significant areas of overlap, especially when the different causal variables are considered one at a time and not in combinations.

The values in each column, considered as a set, describe different theoretically based types of subnations. The coding "1" indicates that the perspec-

TABLE 11: Summary Presentation of Predictions of Three Theories
of Ethnic Political Mobilization

| | Guiding Perspective | | |
CHARACTERISTIC	DEVELOPMENTAL	REACTIVE	COMPETITIVE
Size of Subnation (S)	$(1)^a$	$(1)^a$	1
Linguistic Base (L)	1	0	$(1)^a$
Relative Wealth (W)	$(0)^a$	0	1
Economic Status (G)	0	$?^b$	$?^b$

[a]Predictions in parentheses are only weakly indicated by the theories.
[b]Question marks indicate that no clear prediction is made.

tive views the presence of the feature as important; "0" indicates that the perspective views the absence of the feature as important; "?" indicates that no clear position is discernible—the prediction is context-specific; parentheses are used to indicate predictions that are only weakly indicated by the theories.

It is clear from Table 11 what the main concerns of each perspective are; these, in turn, can be represented in Boolean terms. The developmental perspective emphasizes linguistic base and economic status. The image portrayed is that of a culturally distinct, economically isolated subnation. (Using variable names, this is represented as Lg, where uppercase letters indicate presence, lowercase indicate absence, and multiplication indicates logical AND.) The main concerns of the reactive ethnicity perspective, by contrast, center on the predatory behavior of the dominant cultural group. Thus, this perspective emphasizes the damage inflicted on the subnation's language and economy (lw). Finally, the ethnic competition perspective emphasizes the power of the subnation vis-à-vis the core cultural group. Size and wealth are important because these are the resources that increase the likelihood that mobilization will bear fruit (SW).

The next step of the Boolean analysis is to construct a truth table with data on subnations, using the four variables described above and an outcome variable. In this analysis the outcome is ethnic political mobilization as indicated by several possible achievements: the formation of an ethnic political party, the mobilization of a substantial membership or following, election of representatives to national or regional legislative assemblies, and initiating other forms of political action (demonstrations, ethnic political violence, and the like). Subnations were sorted into three categories of ethnic political mo-

TABLE 12: Data on Territorially Based Linguistic Minorities of Western Europe

Minority	S	L	W	G	E
Lapps, Finland	0	0	0	0	0
Finns, Sweden (Torne Valley)	0	0	0	0	0
Lapps, Sweden	0	0	0	0	0
Lapps, Norway	0	0	0	0	0
Albanians, Italy	0	0	0	0	0
Greeks, Italy	0	0	0	0	0
North Frisians, Germany	0	0	0	1	1
Danes, Germany	0	0	0	1	1
Basques, France	0	0	0	1	1
Ladins, Italy	0	0	1	0	0
Magyars, Austria	0	1	0	0	0
Croats, Austria	0	1	0	0	0
Slovenes, Austria	0	1	0	0	1
Greenlanders, Denmark	0	1	0	0	1
Aalanders, Finland	0	1	1	0	2
Slovenes, Italy	0	1	1	1	1
Valdotians, Italy	0	1	1	1	2
Sards, Italy	1	0	0	0	1
Galicians, Spain	1	0	0	0	1
West Frisians, Netherlands	1	0	0	1	1
Catalans, France	1	0	0	1	1
Occitans, France	1	0	0	1	1
Welsh, Great Britain	1	0	0	1	2
Bretons, France	1	0	0	1	2
Corsicans, France	1	0	0	1	2
Friulians, Italy	1	0	1	1	1
Occitans, Italy	1	0	1	1	1
Basques, Spain	1	0	1	1	2
Catalans, Spain	1	0	1	1	2
Flemings, France	1	1	0	0	1
Walloons, Belgium	1	1	0	1	2
Swedes, Finland	1	1	1	0	2
South Tyroleans, Italy	1	1	1	0	2
Alsatians, France	1	1	1	1	1
Germans, Belgium	1	1	1	1	2
Flemings, Belgium	1	1	1	1	2

S = Size of subnation
L = Linguistic ability
W = Relative wealth of subnation
G = Growth vs. decline of subnational region
E = Degree of ethnic political mobilization

bilization (E): little or no evidence of mobilization (0), some evidence of mobilization (1), and considerable evidence of mobilization (2).

Table 12 reports the different combinations of values for thirty-six subnations and their scores on the crude mobilization measure. Thus, $S = 1$ if the subnation is large; $L = 1$ if members of the subnation speak and write the minority language; $W = 1$ if the subnation is as rich as or richer than the larger nation; $G = 1$ if immigration into the subnation exceeds emigration from the subnation; $E = 2$ if there is substantial evidence of ethnic political mobilization; $E = 1$ if there is at least some evidence of ethnic political mobilization; otherwise $E = 0$.

The first major task is to code a single dichotomous outcome (1 or 0) for all cases conforming to each combination of causal conditions. As noted in Chapter 7, if the cases conforming to a certain combination of values do not show clear tendencies, then some method for resolving the contradiction must be devised. The data presented above present no ambiguous combinations of values. The one possibly troublesome combination is the coincidence of small size, weak linguistic base, low relative wealth, and economic advance (0001). The three cases that display these values (North Frisians and Danes in Germany and Basques in France) all display some evidence of ethnic political mobilization, but not strong evidence. Generally, a combination of input values was not coded as a positive instance of ethnic political mobilization in the Boolean analysis unless half of the cases conforming to the combination displayed clear evidence of mobilization (that is, had scores of 2 in Table 12). There were no combinations that embraced cases with little mobilization (0) and clear evidence of mobilization (2). Thus, the one troublesome combination of values was coded 0 (little or no evidence of mobilization). The resulting truth table, with ethnic political mobilization (E) coded as a presence/absence dichotomy, is presented in Table 13.

Table 13 summarizes the different combinations of conditions associated with ethnic political mobilization among Western European subnations. Application of the minimization algorithms described in Chapters 6 and 7 to the truth table (treating nonexistent combinations as instances of no ethnic mobilization) results in the following logically minimal reduced Boolean expression for instances of ethnic political mobilization. In the equations that follow, a variable name in uppercase letters indicates that it must be present (1); a variable name in lowercase letters indicates that it must be absent (0).

$$E = SG + LW$$

TABLE 13: Truth Table Representation of Data on Causes
of Ethnic Political Mobilization

S	L	W	G	E	N
0	0	0	0	0	6
0	0	0	1	0	3
0	0	1	0	0	1
0	0	1	1	?	0
0	1	0	0	0	4
0	1	0	1	?	0
0	1	1	0	1	1
0	1	1	1	1	2
1	0	0	0	0	2
1	0	0	1	1	6
1	0	1	0	?	0
1	0	1	1	1	4
1	1	0	0	0	1
1	1	0	1	1	1
1	1	1	0	1	2
1	1	1	1	1	3

S = Size of subnation
L = Linguistic ability
W = Relative wealth of subnation
G = Growth vs. decline of subnational region
E = Degree of ethnic political mobilization

The reduced equation indicates that there are two basic combinations of conditions linked to ethnic political mobilization. The first combines large size and economic advance (more immigration than emigration); the second combines strong linguistic base and high relative wealth. It is possible at this point to apply De Morgan's Law to this result to produce an equation (with e in lowercase to denote absence) describing the subnations that fail to mobilize:

$$e = (s + g)(l + w)$$
$$= sl + sw + gl + gw$$

The equation is most consistent with the ethnic competition perspective because it shows that subnations which suffer more than one deficiency (from a resource mobilization point of view) are not likely to mobilize. The only pairs of deficiencies that subnations can possess and still mobilize are *lw* and *sg*, as we shall see.

Several features of this analysis should be noted. First, the equation for the presence of ethnic political mobilization ($E = SG + LW$) is logically minimal. Using the procedures outlined in Chapter 7 for incorporating simplifying assumptions does not result in a simpler solution. Second, all prime implicants produced in the first phase of the algorithm appear in the final reduced equation. Thus, there are no prime implicants that were eliminated by applying the prime implicant chart procedure. (As noted in Chapter 7, these considerations are important because they are relevant to the issue of parsimony.)

At first glance, the equation for the presence of ethnic political mobilization (E) offers greatest support for the ethnic competition perspective. Although neither term reproduces the core prediction of this perspective (SW), both terms are compatible with this perspective because the images they evoke are those of powerful subnations with the resources necessary for challenging the core cultural group. Not all is lost, however, for the other perspectives. It is important at this stage of the investigation to apply the techniques for evaluating theories outlined in Chapter 7. To simplify the presentation, the three theories are examined one at a time, not in a combined equation.

The core of the reactive ethnicity argument, at least as outlined above, emphasizes low relative wealth (w) and a weak linguistic base (l). These expectations derive from a theoretically based interest in the predatory actions of core cultural groups. Using the techniques outlined in Chapter 7, it is possible to identify subnations that conform to both the predictions of the reactive ethnicity perspective (designated by R, for reactive ethnicity) and the equation derived for ethnic political mobilization (E). This set is formed from the intersection of R and E:

$$R = lw$$
$$E = SG + LW$$
$$R(E) = SlwG$$

Thus, the two equations (the equation derived from the reactive ethnicity perspective and the equation modeling the results of the analysis of ethnic political mobilization) intersect. The term that results from their intersection combines large size, weak linguistic base, low relative wealth, and economic advance. A total of six subnations conform to this combination of conditions. They are West Frisians (Netherlands), Catalans (France), Occitans (France), Bretons (France), Corsicans (France), and Welsh (Great Britain).

Two conclusions follow from this result. First, the reactive ethnicity perspective (at least as presented above) is incomplete in the specification of conditions likely to generate ethnic political mobilization. Peripheralization (specifically, the lw combination) is linked to ethnic political mobilization only among larger subnations experiencing economic advance. As noted, economic advance might indicate disruption of an existing cultural division of labor (a condition emphasized by the ethnic competition perspective; see Ragin 1979) or a new interest in the resources of the peripheral region by the core cultural group. Second, the reactive ethnicity perspective can be usefully applied to these six subnations by using the $SlwG$ combination to guide the analysis and interpretation of these six cases.

One conflict in the study of ethnic political mobilization over the last few years has concerned the applicability of the three major perspectives to Wales. Alford (1963), Cox (1967, 1970), and Butler and Stokes (1969) applied the developmental perspective. Hechter (1975) applied the reactive ethnicity perspective. And I have applied the ethnic competition perspective (Ragin 1977, 1979, 1986; Ragin and Davies 1981). The results presented here indicate that when viewed in comparative perspective a combination of the last two theories may be usefully applied to this case.

These same procedures can be used to evaluate the ethnic competition perspective. This perspective (designated C) emphasizes resources of size and wealth (SW). The Boolean interesection of this theoretically based expectation with the final equation for E shows that their area of overlap is

$$C = SW$$
$$E = SG + LW$$
$$C(E) = SWG + SLW$$
$$= SW(G + L)$$

The equation states simply that ethnic political mobilization occurs when large size and greater relative wealth are combined with either economic advance or strong linguistic base. Referring back to the original data reveals that a larger number of subnations are covered by the intersection equation based on the ethnic competition perspective than are covered by the intersection equation based on the reactive ethnicity perspective. Altogether, nine subnations are covered by this intersection equation: Germans (Belgium),

Flemings (Belgium), Swedes (Finland), Alsatians (France), Friulians (Italy), Occitans (Italy), South Tyroleans (Italy), Basques (Spain), and Catalans (Spain).

Again, two conclusions are immediately apparent. First, the ethnic competition perspective is incompletely specified. Large size and greater relative wealth are linked to ethnic political mobilization only in the presence of either economic advance or a strong linguistic base. Thus, the intersection equation provides a basis for elaborating this perspective. Both economic advance and strong linguistic base are resources that undoubtedly enhance ethnic political mobilization. Second, with these refinements the perspective can be applied usefully to nine subnations.

Finally, these same procedures can be used to evaluate the developmental perspective (designated D). This perspective emphasizes strong linguistic base and economic decline (Lg). Intersection with the equation for E shows

$$D = Lg$$
$$E = SG + LW$$
$$D(E) = LWg$$

The intersection equation for the developmental perspective states that when a strong linguistic base is combined with high relative wealth and economic decline, ethnic political mobilization occurs. A total of three subnations conform to this combination: Aalanders (Finland), Swedes (Finland), and South Tyroleans (Italy). Note, however, that two of these subnations (Swedes in Finland and South Tyroleans in Italy) are also covered by the intersection equation for the ethnic competition perspective. Furthermore, the combination of conditions that these two subnations share (large size, strong linguistic base, greater relative wealth, and economic decline) give the impression not of an isolated, peripheral cultural minority (the image conveyed in the developmental perspective) but of a resource-rich, competitive minority (the image presented in the ethnic competition perspective). Thus, these two subnations should be treated as instances of ethnic political mobilization covered by the ethnic competition perspective. This leaves one subnation uniquely covered by the intersection equation for the developmental perspective: Aalanders in Finland. Note that this subnation is *physically* isolated from its larger nation (Finland), a characteristic highly compatible with the logic of the developmental perspective.

Two conclusions follow. First, the combination of a strong linguistic base and economic decline stimulates ethnic political mobilization only in the presence of greater relative wealth. Thus, the range of conditions consistent with developmental logic is narrow. Second, the developmental perspective can be usefully applied to the one case that clearly conforms to this combination.

Finally, it is useful to derive an equation for subnations that exhibit ethnic political mobilization but were not hypothesized to do so by any of the three theories. This equation can be derived by deducing the intersection of the equation for E with the negation of the equation for all subnations hypothesized by any of the three perspectives to display ethnic mobilization. The term H is used to designate such subnations and is formed simply by applying logical OR to the three hypothesis equations given above. The negation of hypothesized instances (which would show subnations not hypothesized to exhibit ethnic political mobilization and is designated h) is derived by applying De Morgan's Law to the equation for hypothesized instances:

$$H = lw + SW + Lg$$
$$h = (L + W)(s + w)(l + G)$$
$$= slW + sLG + sWG + LwG$$
$$h(E) = (slW + sLG + sWG + LwG)(SG + LW)$$
$$= sLWG + SLwG$$

There are surprisingly few subnations with ethnic political mobilization that were not hypothesized by one of the three perspectives to display mobilization. There are two instances of the first term, which combines small size, strong linguistic base, high relative wealth, and economic advance: Slovenes of Italy and Valdotians of Italy. There is only one instance of the second term, which combines large size, strong linguistic base, lower relative wealth, and economic advance: Walloons of Belgium. The first two cases both exist as subnations because of relatively unusual historical circumstances. The Walloons of Belgium in many respects are not a subnation (they are the dominant cultural group in Belgium) and have mobilized as an ethnic group partially in response to Flemish mobilization. Thus, it is possible to account for these theoretical outliers by citing additional historical and political evidence.

SUMMARY.   Overall, the results indicate that the reactive ethnicity and ethnic competition perspectives are both applicable to a substantial number of instances of ethnic political mobilization. Consistent with the results of the case studies cited above, it is apparent that the developmental perspective is not a useful tool for understanding contemporary ethnic mobilization in Western Europe. The reactive ethnicity perspective is applicable to six cases at most, while the ethnic competition perspective is applicable to nine cases and probably to some of the cases covered by the reactive ethnicity perspective (such as Wales), as well.

To some extent it is surprising that the reactive ethnicity perspective, even in its emended form, is applicable to many Western European subnations. One is surprised for two reasons. First, Western Europe has had formally constituted, modern nation-states on its soil for centuries. There have been many boundary changes over this period, and subnations have been created in the wake of these changes. Most of these subnations were spared demotion to the status of internal colony. Thus, the historical conditions surrounding the formation of many Western European subnations do not conform well to the scenario outlined in the reactive ethnicity perspective. Second, in most of Western Europe industrialization preceded or accompanied democratization. Thus, the class cleavage was favored in the development and maturation of these polities (Lipset and Rokkan 1967; Rokkan 1970). This sequence of events may have stunted the mobilization of ethnic lower strata as ethnic as opposed to class collectivities. Consistent with this historical pattern, it should be noted that of the six subnations covered by the reactive ethnicity perspective, five traditionally have displayed relatively high levels of voting for socialist and social democratic parties. Thus, these subnations have tended to mobilize along class lines in concert with polity-wide efforts (see Ragin and Davies 1981; Ragin 1986).

The results indicate that both of the major perspectives, as initially specified, are incomplete. The intersection equations show the shortcomings of these theories quite explicitly. The ethnic competition perspective, as formulated, ignores the importance of having either economic advance or strong linguistic base coincide with large size and relative wealth. The reactive ethnicity perspective ignores the fact that large size and economic advance must accompany the conditions it emphasizes (weak linguistic base and low relative wealth) for ethnic mobilization to occur. The more elaborate versions of these perspectives, presented in the intersection equations $R(E)$ and $C(E)$, should be used as guides when interpreting specific cases.

The goal of interpreting cases is important. Boolean-based techniques of qualitative comparison are not used simply to assess multiple conjunctural causation or to evaluate theories, but also to establish a strong comparative foundation for interpretive analysis of specific cases or sets of cases. Thus, the completion of this study of ethnic political mobilization would involve further specification of these two types of ethnic political mobilization (the reactive type and the competitive type) and the elaboration of a more detailed account of mobilization in specific cases. This would entail use of the method of agreement to establish further similarities among the cases conforming to each type and, further, use of the method of difference to refine the specification of differences between types (see Chapter 3). Essentially, the Boolean analysis establishes the important signposts for a more detailed investigation of ethnic mobilization in Western Europe.

The results support the idea that there is great diversity among subnations and among instances of ethnic political mobilization. It is not possible to embrace all instances within a single framework. In some respects, this conclusion is too easy, for it simply affirms that there is a great deal of complexity to social phenomena, a conclusion that few would challenge. The Boolean analysis does more than simply confirm complexity, however. It shows the key combinations of causal conditions linked to ethnic political mobilization. It maps the complexity of ethnic mobilization and provides a basis for limited generalization and further investigation.

APPLICATION TO EMPIRICAL TYPOLOGIES OF ORGANIZATIONS

Empirical typologies are valuable because they are formed from interpretable combinations of values of theoretically or substantively relevant variables which characterize the members of a general class. The different combinations of values are seen as representing types of the general phenomenon. (See Barton 1955 : 40–45 for an early discussion of basic principles of empirical typology; see also McKinney 1965, Simon 1969 : 292–300, and Diesing 1971 : 197–202.) Empirical typologies are best understood as a form of social scientific shorthand. A single typology can replace an entire system of variables and interrelations. The relevant variables together compose a multidimensional attribute space; an empirical typology pinpoints specific locations within this space where cases cluster. The ultimate test of an empirical typology is the degree to which it helps social scientists (and, by implication, their audiences) comprehend the diversity that exists within a general class of social phenomena.

The third application of Boolean techniques involves using them to construct an empirical typology. The data used in this example describe organizations (juvenile courts in the United States) and are thus on a smaller scale than the data used in the previous examples (though still macrosocial). The problem is to construct an empirical typology of these courts, a model of their diversity. Thus no causal outcome, per se, is examined. The techniques presented are not limited to organizations. Similar techniques could be used, for example, to develop an empirical typology of Third World countries using criteria specified in dependency theories. The result would be a specification of types of dependent countries, an important issue in the study of dependency and development.

The Boolean approach is appropriate for constructing typologies because it explicitly examines combinations of characteristics and produces a logically minimal statement describing their diversity. In this example, the Boolean analysis addresses the question "how are juvenile courts organized?" by examining the different combinations of organizational features that they exhibit. The analysis is relevant to theories about organizations because it addresses limitations on the variety of organizational forms evident among instances of one type of organization, juvenile courts.

To structure the discussion, the work of Stapleton and others (1982) is extended and elaborated. Stapleton and colleagues develop an empirical typology of juvenile courts using relatively conventional techniques: factor analysis, to identify underlying dimensions of variation among juvenile courts, and cluster analysis to identify key locations in the multidimensional attribute space formed by these underlying dimensions. After reviewing their work, I reanalyze their data by using Boolean techniques.

STAPLETON AND COLLEAGUES' EMPIRICAL TYPOLOGY. Much of the literature on American juvenile courts portrays them as varying along a single traditional–due process continuum (Handler 1965; Dunham 1966; Stapleton and Teitelbaum 1972; Erikson 1974; Tappan 1976; Cohen and Kluegel 1978). While recent contributions have noted that juvenile courts range from all-inclusive bureaucracies to a variety of decentralized structures, the conception of these courts as varying along a single continuum has persisted. Stapleton and colleagues (1982) argue that a unidimensional characterization of juvenile courts neglects both the intricacy of their organizational differences and the different normative systems and work expectations such features reflect.

TABLE 14: Results of Stapleton and Colleagues' Factor Analysis

Factor	Description	Key Indicator/Highest Loading Variable
1	Status offenders processed/scope (S)	Intake or probation officer can refer status offender to voluntary agency
2	Centralization of authority (C)	Court or judge administers probation department
3	Formalization of procedure (F)	Mandatory interval between adjudication and disposition exists and can be formally waived
4	Task specification/differentiation (T)	Prosecutor must be involved in the decision to file a formal petition
5	Discretion (D)	Intake or probation staff may arrange informal probation for law violators

Source: Based on Stapleton and others (1982 : tables 1 and 2).

Stapleton and colleagues conducted factor analyses of 96 dichotomously coded characteristics of 150 metropolitan juvenile courts in order to provide a basis for developing an empirical typology. The basic assumption of the factor analytic approach is that observed correlations between variables are the result of underlying regularities in the data and that any variation in the data which is peculiar to single variables does not reflect general, shared features. The five interpretable factors they found are summarized in Table 14.

The indicator for factor 1 (scope) indicates the courts which have jurisdiction over status offenders. Overall, variables loading on this factor distinguish juvenile courts with jurisdiction over the adjudication and disposition of cases involving status offenders from those lacking such jurisdiction. The key indicator for factor 2 (centralization) concerns the power of the central executive. This variable indicates its control over the probation department. Other variables on this factor also concern subinstitutional loci of decision making. The indicator for factor 3 (formalization) indicates that a mandatory interval between adjudication and disposition exists and that it can be formally waived. Many juvenile courts do not bifurcate adjudication and disposition and thus have less formalized proceedings. The indicator for factor 4 (task specificity) concerns specificity of positions within the court. The participation of the prosecuter in the decision to file formal petitions indicates greater task specificity. The indicator for factor 5 (discretion) assesses intake discretion—how cases are screened prior to court appearance. The indicator distinguishes juvenile courts with greater discretion assigned to staff.

In order to assess the degree to which juvenile courts form interpretable clusters, Stapleton and colleagues selected these five indicators to serve for the five factors in cluster analyses. This procedure ensured the maximum homogeneity within clusters and at the same time minimized the number of clusters because all five variables used to cluster courts were presence/absence dichotomies. Stapleton and colleagues used an agglomerative hierarchical clustering technique (Johnson 1967) and allowed no distance between cases within each cluster. This procedure, which is equivalent to a simple sorting of cases into their different combinations of values on the five dichotomous variables, produced initial clusters. Stapleton and coworkers found a total of twenty-five different combinations of values represented in the data, a number not dramatically smaller than the thirty-two (2^5) logically possible combinations of five dichotomies. Of these twenty-five combinations of values, however, only twelve contained three or more courts. Stapleton and colleagues regarded these twelve as substantively important; thus, thirteen residual clusters and twenty deviant courts were eliminated from further consideration.

The twelve clusters delineated by Stapleton and colleagues supported the received notion that there are two major types of juvenile courts, but they also revealed substantial variation within the two main types and several additional types, as well. Table 15 reports these twelve clusters. Courts in clusters 1 through 4 ($N = 68$) approximate the traditional juvenile court system. These courts combine inclusivity, highly centralized authority, and a low degree of formalization. Courts in clusters 5 and 6 ($N = 7$) were treated by Stapleton and colleagues as a variation of this basic type, the important distinction being that courts in clusters 5 and 6 did not have inclusive jurisdictions. Courts in clusters 7 through 9 ($N = 38$) were considered representative of the decentralized, due process juvenile court—the polar ideal type. In these courts, authority was not centralized and task specificity was high. Courts in cluster 10 ($N = 4$) were treated as a variation of the due process type, similar in most respects to courts in cluster 9. Finally, courts in clusters 11 and 12 were considered to be historical artifacts—the consequence of an atypical regional (mostly New York State) legal system. These last two clusters were not considered representative of either major type and therefore were treated as residual.

Thus, Stapleton and colleagues delineate five aggregate clusters (composed of simple clusters 1–4, 5–6, 7–9, 10, and 11–12) and show that most (82 percent) of the 130 courts examined in the cluster analysis fall at either

TABLE 15: Results of Stapleton and Colleagues' Cluster Analysis

		Structural Dimensions			
CLUSTER NUMBER[a]	SCOPE OF JURISDICTION (S)	CENTRALIZA- TION OF AUTHORITY (C)	FORMAL- IZATION (F)	TASK SPECI- FICATION (T)	INTAKE DISCRETION (D)
1 (32)	Inclusive	High	Low	Low	High
2 (16)	Inclusive	High	Low	High	High
3 (7)	Inclusive	High	Low	High	Low
4 (13)	Inclusive	High	Low	Low	Low
5 (3)	Exclusive	High	Low	High	High
6 (4)	Exclusive	High	Low	Low	High
7 (20)	Inclusive	Low	Low	High	High
8 (14)	Inclusive	Low	High	High	High
9 (4)	Exclusive	Low	Low	High	Low
10 (4)	Exclusive	High	Low	High	Low
11 (4)	Inclusive	Low	Low	Low	Low
12 (9)	Inclusive	Low	Low	Low	High

[a]Frequency is given in parentheses.

end of the traditional–due process continuum (in aggregate clusters 1–4 or 7–9). They also identify the key features of both major types of courts. In traditional juvenile courts, the scope of jurisdiction is wide; authority is centralized; and there is a low degree of formalization. In due process juvenile courts, authority is decentralized and task specificity is high. While these two polar types predominate, Stapleton and colleagues show substantial variation within each of these two types, and they show additional types as well. They conclude that bipolar conceptions of juvenile courts, though valuable, are simplistic.

While Stapleton and colleagues' treatment of types of juvenile courts is thorough and convincing, their procedures for transforming the twelve simple clusters (the most frequent combinations of scores) into five aggregate clusters or types do not follow any specific methodological guidelines. Yet the major conclusions of their paper rest on these aggregate clusters, not on the twelve simple clusters pinpointed in the rudimentary cluster analysis. They emphasize the contrast between aggregate clusters 1–4 and 7–9 because these two constitute the two major types—traditional and due process. Yet there are no strong methodological arguments offered for grouping the simple clusters in this manner. Ultimately, their specification of aggregate clusters rests on a general, theoretically based expectation that at least these two dominant types should emerge.

A BOOLEAN APPROACH TO EMPIRICAL TYPOLOGY.   Boolean techniques offer a more structured approach to the construction of empirical typologies. These techniques can be used to compare clusters holistically and to identify their key underlying differences. The goal of Boolean analysis here is to produce aggregate clusters, or types, from the simple clusters reported by Stapleton and colleagues (which resulted from sorting cases into their different combinations of scores). The Boolean approach is appropriate because it provides explicit, logical rules for simplifying complexity. This feature converges with the purpose of empirical typology: to provide a useful shorthand for describing the diversity that exists within a given class of social phenomena. In the Boolean approach, the fully reduced Boolean equation that results from application of the minimization algorithms to a truth table specifies the combinations of characteristics defining each major type. In short, this technique pinpoints essential combinations of characteristics in a way that logically summarizes the diversity displayed in the truth table.

Stapleton and colleagues' twelve clusters (presented above) can be used to construct a truth table, as shown in Table 16. The column headings refer to the five structural variables. The output (E) indicates whether or not a certain combination of features is found in at least three courts. This truth table is a faithful reproduction of the results of Stapleton and colleagues' simple clusters. Stapleton and coworkers used five dichotomies to identify twelve clusters of juvenile courts. They used a frequency criterion of three to distinguish substantively important clusters from unimportant clusters. All that has been added is an output code (1 indicates that the combination of values exists with sufficient frequency to be considered significant by Stapleton and colleagues) and the remaining rows (that is, combinations of values that are infrequent or simply do not exist in the data).

Application of the minimization algorithms presented in Chapters 6 and 7 to this truth table results in the following fully reduced Boolean equation:

$$E(\text{exists}) = Sft + CfT + CfD + ScTD + sfTd$$
Type: 1   2   3   4   5

Variable names in uppercase letters indicate that the characteristic is present (1); variable names in lowercase letters indicate that it is absent (0). Multi-

TABLE 16: Truth Table Representation of Results of Stapleton and Colleagues'
Cluster Analysis

Row	S	C	F	T	D	Combination of Values on Structural Dimensions / Output Value (1 = Frequency > 2) E

Row	S	C	F	T	D	E
1	1	1	0	0	1	1
2	1	1	0	1	1	1
3	1	1	0	1	0	1
4	1	1	0	0	0	1
5	0	1	0	1	1	1
6	0	1	0	0	1	1
7	1	0	0	1	1	1
8	1	0	1	1	1	1
9	0	0	0	1	0	1
10	0	1	0	1	0	1
11	1	0	0	0	0	1
12	1	0	0	0	1	1
13	0	0	0	0	0	0
14	0	0	0	0	1	0
15	0	0	0	1	1	0
16	0	0	1	0	0	0
17	0	0	1	0	1	0
18	0	0	1	1	0	0
19–32	. . . (remaining terms)					0

S = Scope of jurisdiction
C = Centralization
F = Formalization
T = Task specificity
D = Intake discretion
E = Combination exists

plication indicates logical AND; addition (+) indicates logical OR. The sym-
bol S indicates inclusiveness of jurisdiction (1 = inclusive jurisdiction); C
indicates that authority is centralized (1 = high); F indicates degree of formalization of procedures (1 = high); T indicates task specificity (1 = high);
and D indicates intake discretion (1 = high).

The equation delineates five different types of juvenile courts. The first
three types overlap to some degree. The first combines inclusive scope with
a low degree of formalization and a low degree of task specificity. This type
conforms roughly to Stapleton and colleagues' traditional court. Note, however, that this Boolean term embraces not only courts in clusters 1 and 4 but

also those in clusters 11 and 12. Stapleton and colleague's traditional type embraced clusters 1, 2, 3, and 4; 11 and 12 were considered deviant. The second type reported in the equation combines centralized authority with a low degree of formalization and a high degree of task specificity. This type covers courts defined by Stapleton and colleagues as traditional (those in clusters 2, 3, and, to a lesser extent, 5) and courts identified as similar to the due process type (courts in cluster 10). The third type is very similar to the second. It combines centralized authority, a low degree of formalization, and a high degree of intake discretion. Courts covered by this type include courts in clusters 1, 2, 5, and 6. These courts were identified as traditional or as similar to traditional courts by Stapleton and colleagues. With the exception of cluster 6, the courts covered by this type overlap with the courts covered by the first two types. (Although types identified in Boolean analysis are often mutually exclusive, this outcome is not automatic.) Thus, the first three types identified in the Boolean analysis appear to be cousins of the traditional type specified by Stapleton and colleagues.

The fourth type combines four elements: inclusive scope, low centralization of authority, high task specificity, and high intake discretion. This type conforms well to Stapleton and coworkers' description of the due process juvenile court and embraces courts in clusters 7 and 8. The last term in the equation also combines four terms. The elements combined—limited scope, low formalization, high task specificity, and low intake discretion—conform very loosely to what Stapleton and colleagues call the felony justice model, a variation of the due process model. Courts in clusters 9 and 10 conform to this type. These two clusters are treated in a residual manner by Stapleton and coworkers.

Overall, the results of the Boolean analysis of the truth table reported in Table 16 are roughly compatible with Stapleton and colleagues' typology, but there is substantial disagreement. First, courts considered by Stapleton and colleagues to be historical artifacts (those in clusters 11 and 12) are shown to conform to one of the Boolean specifications of the traditional court (type 1). Second, the Boolean analysis shows at least two distinct subtypes of traditional courts (types 1 and 2 in the Boolean equation above), as well as a third traditional type overlapping with the first two. Type 1 courts deviate from the ideal-typic traditional court delineated by Stapleton and colleagues in that these courts may or may not be centralized. Type 2 courts deviate by manifesting a high degree of task specificity, a characteristic usually associated with due process juvenile courts. Also, type 2 courts may or may not be inclusive in scope, a key feature of the ideal-typic traditional court. Type 3 courts, which overlap with type 1 and type 2 courts, also may be either inclusive or exclusive and may or may not have a high level of task specificity. Still, all the clusters of courts conforming to the third type were defined by Stapleton and coworkers as traditional courts or as similar to traditional courts.

The clearest support for Stapleton and colleagues' typology is in the Boolean specification of due process juvenile courts, which included courts in clusters 7 and 8. The elements combined in the fourth type above—inclusiveness, low centralization of authority, high task specificity, and high intake discretion—are all ideal-typic features of due process courts. There is an important incompatibility between the Boolean results and Stapleton and colleagues' typology, however. In the Boolean analysis, cluster 9, a member of Stapleton and coworkers' due process aggregate cluster, is shown to belong to a distinct type. Cluster 9 is grouped with cluster 10 by the Boolean analysis, forming a fifth type.

The Boolean analysis presented above is not entirely satisfactory from a minimization point of view because of the overlap, conceptual and empirical, that exists among the first three types. Furthermore, the analysis also falls short from the perspective of substantive interests because it fails to delineate a coherent traditional type. These shortcomings suggest that the analysis is too fine-grained because far too many types are delineated relative to theoretical expectations. Of course, if the goal of the analysis had been simply to confirm that complexity exists (one of Stapleton and colleagues' goals), then the results are clearly satisfactory. Still, a less fine-grained analysis would be valuable given the expectation in the literature of two main types of juvenile courts.

To produce a less fine-grained Boolean analysis it is necessary simply to alter the frequency criterion used to define substantively important clusters. Stapleton and colleagues use a frequency criterion of three as a cutoff for substantive significance. It easily could be argued that this cutoff is too low, especially considering that slight measurement errors could produce spurious substantive significance. Two of the four courts in Stapleton and colleagues' cluster 9, for example, are included in this cluster "because of measurement error" (Stapleton and others 1982:562). Eliminating these two cases produces a frequency value of two for cluster 9 and a consequent reduction to substantive insignificance.

The frequency data reported by Stapleton and colleagues can be used to select an alternative cutoff value (see Table 15). Specifically, there is a clear gap in the frequency distribution between four and seven. Using four instead of three as the cutoff changes little. Using seven as the cutoff value, however, reclassifies five clusters (numbers 5, 6, 9, 10, and 11) to false (that is, substantive insignificance). By recoding these rows, the truth table in Table 16 is modified so that only the seven high-frequency clusters are coded true (1). This new truth table can be minimized with the same Boolean algorithms applied to the original truth table.

The results of this second Boolean analysis are

$$E(\text{exists}) = SCf + ScTD + SfD$$
Type: 1   2   3

These results differ substantially from those reported for the first Boolean analysis. The first type combines inclusive scope, centralized authority, and a low degree of formalization. Courts conforming to this type (those in clusters 1–4) are clearly traditional. The second type combines inclusive scope, a low degree of centralization, a high degree of task specificity, and a high degree of intake discretion. This combination of traits characterizes due process juvenile courts and embraces those in clusters 7 and 8. The third type crosscuts the other two. It combines inclusive scope, low formalization, and high intake discretion. This type covers courts in clusters 1, 2, 7, and 12. The only cluster covered uniquely by the third type is cluster 12, a cluster that Stapleton and colleagues define as residual, a historical artifact.

This last combination of features, however, should be treated as an overlapping type, not as residual. The image suggested by this type is that of a court with a strong social service orientation. Procedures are informal and some violators are offered "relief from the law" at the discretion of the intake staff (see Stapleton and others 1982 : 555). By treating this third type as an overlapping type, it is possible to differentiate subtypes within the first two types. Within the traditional type, for example, courts in clusters 1 and 2 are social service–traditional courts, while courts in clusters 3 and 4 are nonsocial service–traditional courts. The feature of courts in clusters 3 and 4 that precludes them from being classified as social service–traditional courts is their low level of intake discretion. In a similar manner, courts in cluster 7 are social service–due process courts, while courts in cluster 8 are nonsocial service–due process courts. The feature of courts in cluster 8 that excludes them from the social service–due process category is their high level of formalization. Courts in cluster 12 appear to be pure social service courts, lacking both traditional and due process features.

The results presented above showing the different types that exist can be converted to an explicit Boolean statement of the combinations of organizational characteristics that do not exist or are unlikely. To produce this result, it is necessary simply to apply De Morgan's Law to the last equation modeling the three types:

$$E = SCf + ScTD + SfD$$
$$e = s + cd + Ft + FC$$

The first term in the equation shows that juvenile courts with exclusive scope are rare; most courts process all kinds of offenders. This is not a surprising finding; it is obvious from simple inspection of the frequency distribution for this variable. The other terms are more important from the standpoint of organizational theory because they show combinations of structural characteristics that are unlikely in juvenile courts. These unlikely or rare combinations include decentralization combined with a low level of discretion, a high degree of formalization combined with a low degree of task specificity, and a high degree of formalization combined with a high degree of centralization. From an organizational standpoint, it is possible to view these three pairs of features as structurally antagonistic. Generally, these pairs combine traditional features and due process features. This pattern of results reinforces the view of juvenile courts as either traditional or due process. Note, however, that the fourth term in the equation (formalization with centralization) combines classic features of bureaucracies. The fact that this combination of features (which is in line with the expectations of organizational theory) is unlikely in juvenile courts is consistent with the idea that there is a tension in criminal justice systems between the demands of the day-to-day processing of defendants and their rights.

To summarize: Stapleton and colleagues' analysis indicated that the key features of traditional courts are their inclusive scope, their centralization of authority, and their low level of formalization. These are the three features shared by the four clusters of courts they define as traditional. The Boolean analysis of high-frequency clusters confirms this specification of the traditional type. The due process court, according to Stapleton and colleagues, combines a low level of centralization of authority and a high level of task specificity. These are the features shared by courts in clusters 7–9, their due process aggregate cluster. According to the Boolean analysis of high-frequency clusters, due process courts are also inclusive in scope and have a high level of intake discretion. The Boolean analysis indicates further that courts in cluster 9 do not conform well to the due process type. These courts are exclusive in scope and lack intake discretion. Finally, the Boolean analysis suggests that an overlapping social service type crosscuts the traditional–due process distinction, making it possible to distinguish subtypes of traditional and due process courts.

The Boolean approach to the formulation of empirical typologies offers several distinct advantages. First, it provides explicit procedural rules for identifying types. Second, the Boolean algorithms are logical and holistic in their approach to the task of reducing the complexity represented in the truth table. Third, as shown above, a Boolean analysis can be constructed in a variety of ways—it is flexible. An investigator can choose a finer-grained analysis by selecting a lower-frequency cutoff. A higher criterion value can be chosen if a simpler empirical typology is desired. One apparent drawback of the Boolean approach is that the types identified are not always mutually exclusive. However, this liability can be turned into an additional asset if the investigator anticipates imperfect conformity of cases to types. The empirical world provides many examples of mixed types—cases that combine features of conceptually pure types. Overlapping types identified in Boolean analysis provide a vocabulary for discussing such cases. Finally, using De Morgan's Law, the results of the Boolean analysis can be converted into an explicit statement of structural incompatibilities, a feature which enhances the theoretical relevance of the typology.

With a larger data set, the possibility of interpreting specific cases or categories of cases diminishes. However, the results of the Boolean analyses presented above could be used as a basis for a study of the development of the juvenile justice system in the United States. Most organizations bear the mark of their period of origin (Stinchcombe 1965). It may be that juvenile courts which were formed (or reformed) during the same period are of the same or overlapping types. An investigation of this sort, of course, is far beyond the scope of this brief overview of Boolean techniques of typology construction. It is important to note, however, that the construction of such typologies is rarely the endpoint of an investigation.

LIMITATIONS OF THIS CHAPTER

Currently, mainstream social science methodology favors a predominantly variable-oriented approach to social data, an approach that submerges cases into distributions and correlations. This tendency discourages thinking about cases as wholes—that is, as interpretable combinations of parts. Thus, from the perspective of mainstream social science, the value of Boolean-based comparative analysis is not readily apparent. To view cases as wholes, however, makes it possible to interpret them as cases and thus reestablishes a link between social science and actual entities. In short, these techniques make it possible to maintain an interest in both social science theory and specific empirical instances of the processes that interest social scientists and their audiences.

The examples of Boolean methods of qualitative comparison presented in this chapter barely scratch the surface of potential applications. The first example contrasts Boolean methods with Rokkan's configurational approach in comparative political sociology. The second applies Boolean techniques to the study of ethnic political mobilization in Western Europe and tests three theories in a way that enhances their interpretive value. The third focuses on the general problem of empirical typologies using data on organizations. Many other applications are possible. The techniques are relevant to any investigation that is oriented toward viewing cases or instances as wholes—as combinations of characteristics.

The illustrations of Boolean methods presented in this chapter have several shortcomings. Some of these shortcomings follow directly from the selection of relatively simple examples, but they also reflect certain limitations of the approach. First, as presented, the techniques are limited to categorical data. This limitation contradicts the current preference in mainstream social science for techniques designed for interval-scale data. As I have noted elsewhere, however, the algorithms described here can be adapted to interval-scale data. These adaptations are not presented because they are complex, and they obscure my primary goal—to demonstrate and formalize the unique features and strengths of qualitative, holistic comparison and begin to bridge the gulf between variable-oriented and case-oriented research.

The second shortcoming is related to the first. A variety of statistical techniques specifically designed for categorical data and the analysis of complex statistical interaction have been introduced in the social sciences over the last decade. These include log-linear models, logit and probit models, and logistic regression (see Fienberg 1985). This chapter does not address the relation between these techniques and Boolean methods. In general, these statistical techniques require large numbers of cases, especially when statistical interaction is examined. The Boolean methods are designed specifically for analyses involving limited numbers of cases. Moreover, when examining statistical interaction these techniques approach the problem hierarchically. Thus, they are biased toward simpler models (a characteristic that many researchers find desirable). Boolean techniques, by contrast, start by assuming maximum complexity. These statistical techniques are further incapacitated by highly collinear interaction terms—when two interaction terms of the same order, for example, explain the same section of variation in the outcome variable. Boolean techniques do not share this liability. Yet even when statistical techniques successfully identify higher-order interaction, it is sometimes difficult to locate it in specific cells or sets of cells in a multiway cross-tabulation. Boolean techniques provide a direct route to this identification and provide a basis for contrasting specific theoretical expectations with specific patterns of interaction. This characteristic suggests a possible future direction: Boolean techniques and these statistical techniques might be usefully combined in studies with large numbers of observations. A preliminary analysis contrasting Boolean techniques and logistic regression has been presented elsewhere (Ragin and others 1984).

Third, the examples emphasize the compatibility of Boolean methods with the goal of interpretation; yet none of the examples takes on the task of interpreting specific cases or historical processes. This restriction exists primarily because of space limitations but also because extensive interpretation of cases (in the discussion of ethnic political mobilization, for example) would detract from the main goal of the work—to address methods of qualitative comparison.

The fourth shortcoming concerns the fact that the examples presented start with truth tables. In actuality, one of the most demanding aspects of the qualitative comparative approach is the construction of useful truth tables. A great deal of intellectual energy must be devoted to selecting appropriate causal variables and studying individual cases before a worthwhile truth table can be constructed.

Fifth, the examples presented are relatively static. This feature contradicts the emphasis on Boolean analysis as an aid to comparative *historical* analysis. Note that it is possible to include causal variables relevant to historical process in a truth table (such as "class mobilization preceded ethnic mobilization," true or false?) and to analyze combinations of such dichotomies. This strategy would enhance the usefulness of Boolean techniques as aids to comparative historical interpretation. It is also possible to investigate comparable outcomes in a single case (such as the causes of regime changes in a single, coup-ridden Third World country) or to pool comparable outcomes in a single country with those of comparable countries (such as the causes of general strikes in several Western European countries). Characteristics specific to historical periods can be included as causes in the analysis of comparable events, both within and between cases.

The final chapter summarizes the special strengths of Boolean methods of qualitative comparison.

The Dialogue of Ideas and Evidence in Social Research

The folklore of mainstream social science is that investigators engage in research so that they can test theories. On the basis of theoretical ideas, hypotheses are formulated; data relevant to the hypotheses are gathered; and the hypotheses are subjected to a test. The hypotheses are rejected or not rejected on the basis of an examination of the evidence. According to this folklore, there is an intentional gulf between concept and hypothesis formation, on the one hand, and data analysis on the other, at least at a formal level. This model of social science dictates that hypotheses be formulated in isolation from data used to test hypotheses. To alter a hypothesis on the basis of data analyses which are also used to test the theory violates the principles of hypothesis testing central to the official logic of mainstream social scientific methods.

In practice, however, no such intentional gulf between hypothesis or concept formation and data analysis usually exists. Most findings, at least most interesting findings, usually result from some form of grounded concept and hypothesis formation based on preliminary data analyses. In other words, most hypotheses and concepts are refined, often reformulated, after the data have been collected and analyzed. Initial examinations of data usually expose the inadequacy of initial theoretical formulations, and a dialogue, of sorts, develops between the investigator's conceptual tools for understanding the data and the data analysis itself. The interplay between concept formation and data analysis leads to progressively more refined concepts and hypotheses. Preliminary theoretical ideas may continue to serve as guides, but they are often refined or altered, sometimes fundamentally, in the course of data analysis.

The nature of the dialogue that develops between theoretical ideas and data analysis is shaped in part by the nature of the methods of data analysis used. From this point of view, social science methodology does not concern mere technique; it concerns the relationship between thinking and researching. The key concern here is the impact of the organization of the investigation and the structure of the data analysis on how the investigator thinks about the subject.

IDEAS AND EVIDENCE IN VARIABLE-ORIENTED AND CASE-ORIENTED RESEARCH

In most studies using variable-oriented techniques, the goal is to demonstrate that a relationship holds for a certain population, and data are collected from that population accordingly. Initial data analyses may show, however, that the relationship does not exist. The investigator may suspect that the key variables are measured improperly—or that the relationship is hidden by other variables or that the functional form of the relationship is not specified correctly—and may experiment with different ways of computing what is essentially the same analysis. Thus, in the typical variable-oriented study, discussions of measurement alternatives, control variables, functional forms, and other specification issues dominate the dialogue that develops between theoretical ideas and data analysis. This is true of almost all investigations that rely primarily upon multivariate statistical techniques of data analysis, including statistically based comparative investigations of large sets of countries. Sometimes investigators speculate that a certain relation may differ among the subpopulations that compose a sample or target population and may examine relationships within subpopulations. Even when such analyses are conducted, however, the trait defining the subpopulations may be treated as a categorical variable. Thus, the problem of subpopulations can be conceptualized, however loosely, as an additional specification issue.

Sometimes researchers using variable-oriented methods examine specific cases. This examination is accomplished most often through the study of residuals. A multivariate model provides a basis for identifying cases that do not conform well to theoretically based predictions. Essentially, the investigator computes the gap between actual values of cases on the dependent variable (say, rate of economic growth over a twenty-year period) and the values predicted by a certain model. Cases with large residuals are identified as outliers. The goal of the researcher is to identify what the outliers have in common and use this knowledge as a way to respecify the analysis or to distinguish populations. (Of course, if the populations are suspected in advance, analysis of covariance procedures can be used to test the hypothesis that the subpopulations differ.)

In an analysis of residuals, the predicted values are based on an equation that models general patterns discernible across a large number of cases. This model, in turn, is based on the assumption that a single causal model is appropriate for all cases identified as members of a certain population. Of course, if a single model does not in fact apply to most of the cases included in the analysis, it may be pointless to compute residuals because the parameters estimated in the equation may deviate sharply from those appropriate for the main population of interest.

The important point here is that in the variable-oriented approach cases stand out as worthy of an investigator's attention when they fail to conform to the predictions of a certain model. (And sometimes these outliers are discarded as deviant cases.) Thus, individual cases typically acquire significance *as cases* only relative to general patterns displayed across many cases, not relative to the specific historical, cultural, political, substantive, or theoretical concerns of the investigator.

Altogether, these features of the variable-oriented strategy shape a research dialogue that is variable-centered. This bias enhances the compatibility of this strategy with the goal of addressing abstract theoretical concerns, a clear benefit, but the strategy is less compatible with the goal of interpreting or understanding specific cases or categories of cases. Variables are the main factors in this dialogue, not individual cases.

In the typical case-oriented comparative study, by contrast, the dialogue between concept formation and data analysis is very different because the methods are holistic in nature and attend to combinations of conditions. Investigators see each case as a whole—as a total situation. In this approach the causal significance of a condition often varies by context. In some contexts a certain cause may be relevant to a given outcome; in others it may be unimportant; and in still others the absence of this condition may be causally significant to the outcome. Furthermore, the analysis of the evidence proceeds on a case-by-case basis. Each case is compared and contrasted with other relevant cases, and they are compared as wholes—as ordered and meaningful *combinations* of parts.

These features of case-oriented comparative methods shape a research dialogue that differs dramatically from that characteristic of the variable-oriented strategy. In case-oriented comparative studies, this dialogue centers on issues of divergence and causal heterogeneity. The problem is not to specify a single causal model that fits the data best (the question that dominates the research dialogue in studies using multivariate statistical techniques) but to determine the number and character of the different causal models that exist among comparable cases. The phenomenon to be explained is viewed as an outcome and thus may be more or less constant across relevant observations—in the sense that all cases display roughly the same outcome. Thus, the goal in case-oriented comparative studies is not to explain variation but to account for the differences among instances of a certain outcome.

In short, case-oriented methods make allowances for causal complexity, especially multiple conjunctural causation. This characteristic fundamentally alters the nature of the dialogue between ideas and evidence. Those who use statistical methods often must assume, for example, that the effect of a cause is the same across different contexts, and they are concerned to derive correct estimates of the net effect of a certain causal variable. Those who use case-oriented methods, by contrast, are more concerned with determining when a cause is important and when it is not—they are more interested in determining the different contexts in which a cause has an impact. In this approach, a cause may be important or significant only in a certain context or delimited set of contexts.

The response of case-oriented investigators to contrary evidence is also quite different. To the extent that the goal of interpretation predominates, contrary evidence represents nothing more than the fully anticipated deviation of empirical events from ideal-typic images. These deviations play an important part in accounts of the uniqueness or particularity of historically significant outcomes. From an interpretive standpoint, therefore, the departure of empirical events from theoretical models is not confounding; it is raw material for historical explanation. To the extent that a case-oriented investigation is oriented more toward limited historical generalization, contrary evidence is typically used as a basis for refining, not rejecting, theory. As noted in Chapter 3, investigators often use contrary evidence to delineate subtypes of the phenomenon of interest, which, in turn, provide a basis for elaborating theories.

Both variable-oriented and case-oriented approaches, however, are limited—the former by a simplifed conception of cause (a conception that may be incompatible with historical explanation), the latter by an inability to address large numbers of cases. In many respects, these limitations derive from strengths. The variable-oriented approach allows investigators to digest large numbers of cases. A simplified conception of cause, embodied in assumptions built into statistical models, makes this possible. These assumptions, however, discourage consideration of causal complexity, and the research dialogue is fundamentally altered as a result. The case-oriented approach, by contrast, allows investigators to comprehend diversity and address causal complexity. By considering cases as wholes, it is possible to examine causal processes more directly, to look at them in context. The research dialogue thus centers on intersections of causal conditions. Yet this approach is overwhelmed when there is too much diversity and too many cases to comprehend. Thus, this approach discourages consideration of large numbers of cases and comparably broad generalizations.

The Boolean approach to qualitative comparison presented in this study is a middle road between the two extremes, variable-oriented and case-oriented approaches—it is a middle road between generality and complexity. It allows investigators both to digest many cases and to assess causal complexity. Of necessity, the Boolean approach structures a qualitatively different dialogue between ideas and evidence. This dialogue is both case-oriented and variable-oriented simultaneously.

IDEAS AND EVIDENCE IN QUALITATIVE COMPARATIVE RESEARCH

The Boolean approach is oriented toward cases because it addresses the different combinations of causes relevant to outcomes and allows the investigator to examine cases relative to different causal paths. An important part of the research dialogue in Boolean analysis, therefore, concerns the comparability of cases. By specifying the assignment of cases to different causal paths, the Boolean approach establishes the boundaries of comparability. Thus, Boolean analyses simultaneously identify key cases and key causal conjunctures, which can then be examined in more detailed case-oriented studies. In general, the identification of different causal conjunctures provides a basis for delineating types and subtypes of social phenomena. Specifying types, in turn, establishes the necessary bridge between the diversity that exists in a given category of historical outcomes and social scientists' attempts to produce theoretically relevant generalizations about events and processes around them.

The research dialogue of Boolean analysis is variable-oriented in two ways. Investigators must identify causal variables; these are the basic building blocks of Boolean analysis. Thus, the research dialogue from the outset concerns causal conditions conceived as variables and focuses explicitly on combinations of causal conditions. The Boolean approach is also variable-oriented in its understanding of individual causes. Boolean analyses assess the empirical boundaries of the effects of each causal variable. Thus, a reduced Boolean equation can be used as a basis for elaborating theory. Most theories are vaguely specified; they do not detail their scope conditions (Walker and Cohen 1985). Boolean analysis provides a way to delineate the scope conditions of causal variables specified in competing theories. The task of comparative social science is transformed from one of testing theories against each other—the competition to explain variation—to one of assessing the limits and boundaries of competing perspectives. This quality of Boolean-based comparative research is illustrated in Chapter 8 in the application to comparative ethnic political mobilization.

Both case-oriented and variable-oriented approaches have characteristic responses to the rejection of initial hypotheses by evidence. The typical variable-oriented response is to respecify the analysis (for example, to devise new measures or to use different control variables). The usual case-oriented response is to differentiate subtypes among positive cases or to construct more elaborate conjunctural arguments to distinguish positive cases from troublesome negative cases. In Boolean analysis the dialogue with evidence stimulated by the rejection of initial hypotheses is transformed. The Boolean approach directly implements case-oriented data reduction strategies (differentiating subtypes or constructing more elaborate conjunctural arguments) in the operation of the minimization algorithms. In essence, the work of comparing cases holistically in order to derive appropriately qualified causal statements is performed by the algorithms. But theory is not discarded in the process of identifying key causal conjunctures. Because theory is used to identify causal conditions, it is possible to contrast the results of the Boolean analysis with theoretically based expectations (formulated in Boolean terms). These contrasts reveal the shortcomings of existing theories and also provide an avenue for identifying which theories (appropriately modified) apply to which cases. As shown in Chapter 8 in the analysis of ethnic mobilization, the Boolean analysis may indicate that a theory (in that analysis, the developmental perspective) may apply to only one or two cases (or to no cases) and therefore can be disregarded.

Boolean analysis does not, as a rule, reject theories in the same way that case-oriented or variable-oriented methods reject theories. It could be argued that the Boolean results for ethnic political mobilization presented in Chapter 8 reject all three perspectives because none of the combinations of conditions reported in the final reduced equation conforms perfectly to theoretical expectations. However, this narrow interpretation of the results of Boolean analysis not only violates the spirit of the case-oriented comparative logic that inspires the Boolean approach; it also overlooks the potential for theoretical development and elaboration available through Boolean-based qualitative research.

The final and perhaps most important aspect of the dialogue of ideas and evidence in Boolean-based comparative work is the compatibility of the approach with the goal of interpretation. Historical explanation, especially in comparative social science, most often focuses on issues related to the divergence that is induced by different causal conjunctures. In its most basic form, the variable-oriented approach is not well suited for examining causal conjunctures; the Boolean approach focuses explicitly on conjunctures. This makes it possible to identify cases with specific conjunctures, which in turn establishes a solid foundation for case-oriented elaboration of similarities and differences using the method of agreement and the indirect method of difference. Boolean analysis, per se, is not as connected to empirical cases as traditional case-oriented methods. (In fact, it has many superficial similarities to the variable-oriented approach; for example, the truth table resembles a data matrix.) However, the *results* of Boolean-based analysis provide important signposts for more detailed historical examination of specific cases, using a traditional case-oriented approach.

BOOLEAN ANALYSIS AS A CORRECTIVE

At present, the variable-oriented strategy is gaining in popularity among comparative social scientists, in part because it has enhanced the legitimacy of comparative research. Applications of variable-oriented techniques have become more and more sophisticated and intelligent, and several promising research traditions have emerged (see, for example, Zimmermann 1983). However, this trend threatens to obscure the distinctive strengths of case-oriented comparative methods, with their attention to cases as wholes and to the combinatorial complexities of social causation. The potency of this threat is apparent in attempts to define case-oriented comparative methods as inferior versions of variable-oriented methods (see, for example, Smelser

1976). The danger is that the pressure to transform questions about histori-cally defined outcomes (such as military coups) into broad questions about structural variation (such as systemic strain) will increase, and social scien-tists will become even more detached from their surroundings and from their audiences.

Still, the urge to get the big picture, to generalize, to make broad theo-retical statements, is great. Moreover, the pressure to test, or at least show the utility of, ideas over the widest possible population of observations re-mains. The Boolean approach provides a way to address large numbers of cases without forsaking complexity. It allows social scientists to be broad without forcing them to resort to vague and imprecise generalizations about structural relationships. In short, it provides a needed corrective to the variable-oriented approach. The analyses presented in Chapter 8 show that the Boolean approach moves away from traditional case-oriented methods by focusing on large numbers of cases but retains some of the logic of the case-oriented approach and thereby provides a link to historical interpretation.

The image of comparative social science that inspires the introduction of Boolean techniques is that the field should not be divided into two parts — those who know something about actual empirical cases and those who know something about multivariate statistical techniques. While it is diffi-cult to know a large number of cases well, historically and empirically de-fined questions can be addressed with Boolean techniques. It is not neces-sary to transform all questions about historical outcomes experienced by many countries or regions into questions about relations between structural variables relevant to all or even to most cases. Well-defined questions about the social origins and bases of common outcomes provide a solid starting point for a historically oriented comparative social science.

Bibliography

Alford, Robert. 1963. *Party and Society*. Chicago: University of Chicago Press.

Allardt, Erik. 1966. Implications of within-nation variations and regional imbalances for cross-national research. In *Comparing Nations*, ed. Richard Merritt and Stein Rokkan, 333–348. New Haven: Yale University Press.

———. 1979. *Implications of the Ethnic Revival in Modern Industrialized Society*. Helsinki: Societas Scientiarium Fennica.

Andreski, Stanislav. 1965. *The Uses of Comparative Sociology*. Berkeley: University of California Press.

Armer, Michael. 1973. Methodological problems and possibilities in comparative research. In *Comparative Social Research*, ed. Michael Armer and Allen Grimshaw, 49–79. New York: Wiley.

Armer, Michael, and Allan Schnaiberg. 1972. Measuring individual modernity: A near myth. *American Sociological Review* 37: 301–316.

Bach, Robert. 1977. Methods of analysis in the study of the world economy: A comment on Rubinson. *American Sociological Review* 42: 811–814.

Bailey, Kenneth. 1982. *Methods of Social Research*. New York: Free Press.

Barton, Allen. 1955. The concept of property space in social research. In *The Language of Social Research*, ed. Paul Lazarsfeld and Morris Rosenberg, 40–53. New York: Free Press.

Bendix, Reinhard. 1977. *Nation-Building and Citizenship: Studies of Our Changing Social Order*. Berkeley: University of California Press.

———. 1978. *Kings or People: Power and the Mandate to Rule*. Berkeley: University of California Press.

Bergesen, Albert. 1980. From utilitarianism to the world-system: The shift from the individual to the world as a whole as the primordial unit of analysis. In *Studies of the Modern World-System*, ed. Albert Bergesen, 1–12. New York: Academic Press.

Bonnell, Victoria. 1980. The uses of theory, concepts and comparison in historical sociology. *Comparative Studies in Society and History* 22: 156–173.

Bornschier, Volker, Christopher Chase-Dunn, and Richard Rubinson. 1978. Cross-national evidence of the effects of foreign investment and aid on economic growth and inequality: A survey of findings and a reanalysis. *American Journal of Sociology* 84: 651–683.

Bradshaw, York. 1985. Dependent development in black Africa: A cross-national study. *American Sociological Review* 50: 195–207.

Burawoy, Michael. 1979. *Manufacturing Consent: Changes in the Labor Process Under Monopoly Capitalism*. Chicago: University of Chicago Press.

Butler, David, and Donald Stokes. 1969. *Political Change in Britain*. New York: Saint Martin's Press.

Campbell, Donald, and Julian Stanley. 1966. *Experimental and Quasi-Experimental Designs for Research*. Chicago: Rand McNally.

Cardoso, Fernando Henrique. 1973. Associated-dependent development: Theoretical and practical implications. In *Authoritarian Brazil: Origins, Policies, and Future*, ed. Alfred Stepan, 142–176. New Haven: Yale University Press.

———. 1977. The consumption of dependency theory in the United States. *Latin America Research Review* 12:7–24.

Chase-Dunn, Christopher, Aaron Pallas, and Jeffrey Kentor. 1982. Old and new research designs for studying the world-system: A research note. *Comparative Political Studies* 15:341–356.

Chirot, Daniel, and Charles Ragin. 1975. The market, tradition, and peasant revolt. *American Sociological Review* 40:428–444.

Cohen, Lawrence, and James Kluegel. 1978. Determinants of juvenile court dispositions: Ascriptive and achieved factors in two metropolitan juvenile courts. *Social Forces* 58:146–161.

Cook, Thomas, and Donald Campbell. 1979. *Quasi-Experimentation: Design and Analysis Issues for Field Settings*. Boston: Houghton Mifflin.

Cox, Kevin. 1967. Regional anomalies in the voting behavior of the populations of England and Wales: 1921–1951. Unpublished Ph.D. dissertation, University of Illinois.

———. 1970. Geography, social contexts, and voting behavior in Wales, 1861–1951. In *Mass Politics*, ed. Erik Allardt and Stein Rokkan, 117–159. New York: Free Press.

Cressey, Donald Ray. 1953. *Other People's Money*. Glencoe, Ill.: Free Press.

Czudnowski, Moshe. 1976. *Comparing Political Behavior*. Beverly Hills: Sage.

Delacroix, Jacques, and Charles Ragin. 1978. Modernizing institutions, mobilization, and Third World development: A cross-national study. *American Journal of Sociology* 84:123–150.

Diesing, Paul. 1971. *Patterns of Discovery in the Social Sciences*. Chicago: Aldine.

Drass, Kriss, and J. William Spencer. 1986. Accounting for presentencing recommendations: Typologies and probation officers' theory of office. Unpublished manuscript. Department of Sociology, Southern Methodist University.

Drass, Kriss, and Charles Ragin. 1986. *QCA: A Microcomputer Package for Qualitative Comparative Analysis of Social Data*. Center for Urban Affairs and Policy Research, Northwestern University.

Dumont, Louis. 1970. *Homo Hierarchicus: The Caste System and Its Implications*. Chicago: University of Chicago Press.

Duncan, Otis Dudley. 1984. *Notes on Social Measurement: Historical and Critical*. New York: Russell Sage Foundation.

Dunham, H. Warren. 1966. The juvenile court: Contradictory orientations in processing offenders. In *Juvenile Delinquency: A Book of Readings*, ed. Rose Giallombardo, 381–398. New York: Wiley.

Durkheim, Emile. [1915] 1961. *The Elementary Forms of the Religious Life*. Reprint. New York: Collier.

Easthope, Gary. 1974. *A History of Social Research Methods*. London: Longman.

Eisenstadt, Shmuel. 1966. *Problems in Sociological Theory*. Jerusalem: Academon.

Erikson, Patricia. 1974. The defense lawyer's role in juvenile court: An empirical investigation into judges' and social workers' points of view. *University of Toronto Law Review* 24:126–148.

Etzioni, Amitai, and Fredric Dubow, eds. 1970. *Comparative Perspectives: Theories and Methods*. Boston: Little, Brown.

Evans, Peter. 1979. *Dependent Development: The Alliance of Multinational, State, and Local Capital in Brazil*. Princeton: Princeton University Press.

Fienberg, Stephen. 1985. *The Analysis of Cross-Classified Categorical Data*. Cambridge: MIT Press.

Frank, André Gunder. 1967. *Capitalism and Underdevelopment in Latin America: Historical Studies of Chile and Brazil*. New York: Monthly Review.

———. 1969. *Latin America: Underdevelopment or Revolution*. New York: Monthly Review.

———. 1972. *Lumpenbourgeoisie, Lumpendevelopment: Dependence, Class, and Politics in Latin America*. New York: Monthly Review.

Gee, Wilson. 1950. *Social Science Research Methods*. New York: Appleton.

Geertz, Clifford. 1963. *Old Societies and New States: The Quest for Modernity in Asia and Africa*. New York: Free Press.

Gellner, Ernest. 1969. *Thought and Change*. Chicago: University of Chicago Press.

Giddens, Anthony. 1973. *The Class Structure of the Advanced Societies*. London: Hutchinson.

Goffman, Erving. 1974. *Frame Analysis: An Essay on the Organization of Experience*. Cambridge: Harvard University Press.

Grimshaw, Allen. 1973. Comparative sociology: In what ways different from other sociologies? In *Comparative Social Research: Methodological Problems and Strategies*, ed. Michael Armer and Allen Grimshaw, 3–48. New York: Wiley.

Gurr, Ted Robert. 1970. *Why Men Rebel*. Princeton: Princeton University Press.

———. 1974. Persistence and change in political systems, 1800–1971. *American Political Science Review* 68 : 1482–1504.

Hage, Jerald. 1975. Theoretical decision rules for selecting research designs: The study of nation-states or societies. *Sociological Methods and Research* 4(2).131 165.

Handler, Joel. 1965. The juvenile court and the adversary system; Problems of form and function. *Wisconsin Law Review* (Winter):7–51.

Hannan, Michael. 1979. The dynamics of ethnic boundaries in modern states. In *National Development and the World System: Educational, Economic and Political Change, 1950–1970*, ed. Michael Hannan and John Meyer, 253–277. Chicago: University of Chicago Press.

Harris, Marvin. 1978. *Cannibals and Kings: The Origins of Cultures*. New York: Vintage.

———. 1985. *Good to Eat: Riddles of Food and Culture*. New York: Simon and Schuster.

Hawley, Amos. 1981. *Urban Society: An Ecological Approach*. New York: Wiley.

Hechter, Michael. 1975. *Internal Colonialism: The Celtic Fringe in British National Development*. London: Routledge & Kegan Paul.

Hopkins, Terence, and Immanuel Wallerstein. 1970. The comparative study of national societies. In *Comparative Perspectives: Theories and Methods*, ed. Amitai Etzioni and Fredric Dubow, 183–204. Boston: Little, Brown.

Inkeles, Alex, and David Smith. 1974. *Becoming Modern: Individual Change in Six Developing Countries*. Cambridge: Harvard University Press.

Jenkins, J. Craig. 1983. Resource mobilization theory and the study of social movements. *Annual Review of Sociology* 9 : 527–553.

Johnson, Stephen. 1967. Hierarchical clustering schemes. *Psychometrika* 32: 241–254.

Kidron, Michael, and Ronald Segal. 1981. *The State of the World Atlas*. New York: Simon & Schuster.

Lenski, Gerhard. 1966. *Power and Privilege*. New York: McGraw-Hill.

———. 1974. *Human Societies*. New York: McGraw-Hill.

Lieberson, Stanley. 1985. *Making It Count: The Improvement of Social Research and Theory*. Berkeley: University of California Press.

Lindesmith, Alfred. 1968. *Addiction and the Opiates*. Chicago: Aldine.

Lipset, Seymour, and Stein Rokkan. 1967. *Party Systems and Voter Alignments*. New York: Free Press.

McCarthy, J. D., and M. N. Zald. 1977. Resource mobilization and social movements: A partial theory. *American Journal of Sociology* 82: 1212–1239.

McDermott, Robert. 1985. *Computer-Aided Logic Design*. Indianapolis: Howard W. Sams.

McGowan, Pat. 1985. Pitfalls and promise in the quantitative study of the world-system: A reanalysis of Bergesen and Schoenberg's "Long Waves" of colonialism. *Review: Journal of the Fernand Braudel Center* 8: 477–500.

McHale, Vincent, and Sharon Skowronski. 1983. *Political Parties of Europe*. Westport, Conn.: Greenwood Press.

McKinney, John. 1965. *Constructive Typology and Social Theory*. New York: Appleton-Century-Crofts.

Mann, Michael. 1973. *Consciousness and Action Among the Western Working Class*. London: Humanities.

Marsh, Robert. 1967. *Comparative Sociology: A Codification of Cross-Sectional Analysis*. New York: Harcourt Brace Jovanovich.

Mendelson, Elliot. 1970. *Boolean Algebra and Switching Circuits*. New York: McGraw-Hill.

Merton, Robert. 1973. *The Sociology of Science: Theoretical and Empirical Investigations*. Chicago: University of Chicago Press.

Mill, John Stuart. [1843] 1967. *A System of Logic: Ratiocinative and Inductive*. Toronto: University of Toronto Press.

Moore, Barrington, Jr. 1966. *The Social Origins of Dictatorship and Democracy: Lord and Peasant in the Making of the Modern World*. Boston: Beacon.

Nagel, Ernest. 1961. *The Structure of Science*. New York: Harcourt.

Nagel, Joane, and Susan Olzak. 1982. Ethnic mobilization in new and old states: An extension of the competition model. *Social Problems* 30: 127–143.

———, eds. 1986. *Competitive Ethnic Relations*. New York: Academic Press.

Nielsen, Francois. 1980. The Flemish movement in Belgium after World War II: A dynamic analysis. *American Sociological Review* 45: 76–94.

———. 1985. Toward a theory of ethnic solidarity in modern societies. *American Sociological Review* 50: 133–149.

Nielsen, Francois, and Michael Hannan. 1977. The expansion of national educational systems: Tests of a population ecology model. *American Sociological Review* 42: 479–490.

Nisbett, Richard, and Lee Ross. 1980. *Human Inference: Strategies and Shortcomings of Social Judgement*. Englewood Cliffs, N.J.: Prentice-Hall.

Olzak, Susan. 1982. Ethnic mobilization in Quebec. *Ethnic and Racial Studies* 5: 253–275.

————. 1983. Contemporary ethnic mobilization. *Annual Review of Sociology* 9 : 355–374.

Paige, Jeffrey. 1975. *Agrarian Revolution: Social Movements and Export Agriculture in the Underdeveloped World.* New York: Free Press.

Parsons, Talcott. 1975. Some theoretical considerations on the nature and trends of change of ethnicity. In *Ethnicity: Theory and Experience,* ed. Nathan Glazer and Daniel Moynihan, 56–71. Cambridge: Harvard University Press.

————. 1977. *The Evolution of Societies.* Englewood Cliffs, N.J.: Prentice-Hall.

Petersen, William. 1975. On the subnations of Western Europe. In *Ethnicity: Theory and Experience,* ed. Nathan Glazer and Daniel Moynihan, 177–208. Cambridge: Harvard University Press.

Porter, John. 1970. Some observations on comparative studies. In *Stages of Social Research,* ed. Dennis Forcese and Stephen Richer, 141–154. Englewood Cliffs, N.J.: Prentice-Hall.

Przeworski, Adam, and Henry Teune. 1970. *The Logic of Comparative Social Inquiry.* New York: Wiley-Interscience.

Ragin, Charles. 1977. Class, status, and "reactive ethnic cleavages": The social bases of political regionalism. *American Sociological Review* 42: 438–450.

————. 1979. Ethnic political mobilization: The Welsh case. *American Sociological Review* 44 : 619–635.

————. 1983. Theory and method in the study of dependency and international inequality. *International Journal of Comparative Sociology* 24 : 121–136.

————. 1985. Knowledge and interests in the study of the modern world-system. *Review: Journal of the Fernand Braudel Center* 8 : 451–476.

————. 1986. The impact of Celtic nationalism on class politics in Scotland and Wales. In *Competitive Ethnic Relations,* ed. Joane Nagel and Susan Olzak, 199–219. New York: Academic Press.

Ragin, Charles, and Daniel Chirot. 1984. The world-system of Immanuel Wallerstein: Sociology and politics as history. In *Vision and Method in Historical Sociology,* ed. Theda Skocpol, 276–312. Cambridge: Cambridge University Press.

Ragin, Charles, and Ted Davies. 1981. Welsh nationalism in context. *Research in Social Movements, Conflicts and Change* 4 : 215–233.

Ragin, Charles, and David Zaret. 1983. Theory and method in comparative research: Two strategies. *Social Forces* 61 : 731–754.

Ragin, Charles, Susan Meyer, and Kriss Drass. 1984. Assessing discrimination: A Boolean approach. *American Sociological Review* 49: 221–234.

Rokkan, Stein. 1966. Comparative cross-national research: The context of current efforts. In *Comparing Nations,* ed. Richard Merritt and Stein Rokkan, 3–26. New Haven: Yale University Press.

————. 1970. *Citizens, Elections, Parties.* New York: McKay.

Roth, Charles. 1975. *Fundamentals of Logic Design.* St. Paul: West.

Rubinson, Richard, and Deborah Holtzman. 1981. Comparative dependence and economic development. *International Journal of Comparative Sociology* 20 : 86–101.

Scheuch, Erwin. 1966. Cross-national comparisons using aggregate data: Some substantive and methodological problems. In *Comparing Nations,* ed. Richard Merritt and Stein Rokkan, 131–168. New Haven: Yale University Press.

Shorter, Edward, and Charles Tilly. 1974. *Strikes in France, 1830–1968.* Cambridge: Cambridge University Press.

Simon, Julian. 1969. *Basic Research Methods in Social Science.* New York: Random House.

Skocpol, Theda. 1979. *States and Social Revolutions: A Comparative Analysis of France, Russia, and China.* Cambridge: Cambridge University Press.

Skocpol, Theda, and Margaret Somers. 1980. The uses of comparative history in macrosocial inquiry. *Comparative Studies in Society and History* 22 : 174–197.

Smelser, Neil. 1973. The methodology of comparative analysis. In *Comparative Research Methods,* ed. Donald Warwick and Samuel Osherson, 45–52. Englewood Cliffs, N.J.: Prentice-Hall.

———. 1976. *Comparative Methods in the Social Sciences.* Englewood Cliffs, N.J.: Prentice-Hall.

Snyder, David. 1975. Institutional setting and industrial conflict: Comparative analyses of France, Italy, and the United States. *American Sociological Review* 40 : 259–278.

Stapleton, Vaughn, and Lee Teitelbaum. 1972. *In Defense of Youth: A Study of the Role of Counsel in American Juvenile Courts.* New York: Russell Sage Foundation.

Stapleton, Vaughn, David Aday, and Jeanne Ito. 1982. An empirical typology of American metropolitan juvenile courts. *American Journal of Sociology* 88 : 549–564.

Stephens, John. 1979. *The Transition from Capitalism to Socialism.* London: Macmillan.

Stinchcombe, Arthur. 1961. Agricultural enterprise and rural class relations. *American Journal of Sociology* 67 : 165–176.

———. 1965. Social structure and organizations. In *Handbook of Organizations,* ed. James G. March, 142–193. Chicago: Rand McNally.

———. 1978. *Theoretical Methods in Social History.* New York: Academic Press.

Swanson, Guy. 1971. Frameworks for comparative research: Structural anthropology and the theory of action. In *Comparative Methods in Sociology: Essays on Trends and Applications,* ed. Ivan Vallier, 141–202. Berkeley: University of California Press.

Tappan, Paul. 1976. The nature of juvenile delinquency. In *Juvenile Delinquency: A Book of Readings,* ed. Rose Giallombardo, 5–24. New York: Wiley.

Tilly, Charles. 1975. *The Formation of National States in Western Europe.* Princeton: Princeton University Press.

———. 1978. *From Mobilization to Revolution.* Reading, Mass.: Addison-Wesley.

———. 1984. *Big Structures, Large Processes, Huge Comparisons.* New York: Russell Sage Foundation.

———. 1986. *The Contentious French.* Cambridge, Mass.: Belknap Press.

Tocqueville, Alexis de. [1835] 1945. *Democracy in America.* Reprint. New York: Knopf.

Walker, Henry, and Bernard Cohen. 1985. Scope statements: Imperatives for evaluating theory. *American Sociological Review* 50 : 288–301.

Wallerstein, Immanuel. 1974. *The Modern World System: Capitalist Agriculture and the Origins of the European World Economy in the Sixteenth Century.* New York: Academic Press.

————. 1979. *The Capitalist World-Economy.* Cambridge: Cambridge University Press.

————. 1980. *The Modern World-System II: Mercantilism and the Consolidation of the European World-Economy 1600–1750.* New York: Academic Press.

————. 1984. *The Politics of the World-Economy: The States, the Movements and the Civilizations.* Cambridge: Cambridge University Press.

Walton, John. 1973. Standardized case comparison: Observations on method in comparative sociology. In *Comparative Social Research,* ed. Michael Armer and Allen Grimshaw, 173–188. New York: Wiley.

————. 1984. *Reluctant Rebels.* New York: Columbia University Press.

Weber, Max. 1946. *From Max Weber: Essays in Sociology.* Ed. H. H. Gerth and C. Wright Mills. New York: Oxford University Press.

————. 1949. *The Methodology of the Social Sciences.* New York: Free Press.

————. 1975. *Roscher and Knies: The Logical Problems of Historical Economics.* New York: Free Press.

————. 1977. *Critique of Stammler.* New York: Free Press.

————. 1978. *Economy and Society.* Ed. Guenther Roth and Claus Wittich. Berkeley: University of California Press.

Wiener, Jonathan. 1976. Review of Barrington Moore Jr., "*Social Origins of Dictatorship and Democracy.*" *History and Theory* 15 : 146–175.

Wolf, Eric. 1969. *Peasant Wars of the Twentieth Century.* New York: Harper & Row.

Zelditch, Morris, Jr. 1971. Intelligible comparisons. In *Comparative Methods in Sociology: Essays on Trends and Applications,* ed. Ivan Vallier, 267–307. Berkeley: University of California Press.

Zimmerman, Ekkart. 1983. *Political Violence, Crises, and Revolution: Theory and Research.* Cambridge, Mass.: Schenkman.

Index

Agricultural organization, 75–76
Alford, Robert, 4, 47, 145
Allardt, Erik, 8, 138
Analysis, ix–x, 83, 84, 122
Andreski, Stanislav, 4, 6
Area specialists, ix, 70
Armer, Michael, 2, 4, 53
Assumptions: and the research dialogue, 32–33, 49, 105; of statistical methods, x, xii, 32, 61–64, 103, 105–106, 166, 168; use in Boolean analysis, 105–106, 110–113, 115, 130, 132–133, 144
Audiences, 20–21, 23, 49

Bach, Robert, 8
Bailey, Kenneth, 2
Barton, Allen, 149
BASIC, 123–124
Bendix, Reinhard, 35
Bergesen, Albert, 8
Binary data, 86–87
Bonnell, Victoria, 34, 39
Boole, George, 85
Boolean algebra, viii, xiv, 85–124; addition, 89–91, and data reduction, xi, 92–101; and experimental logic, 93–95; combinatorial logic, 92–93; factoring, 100–101; implication and use of prime implicants, 95–98, 144; limitations, 161–163; minimization, 93–98; multiplication, 91–92; use of binary data, 86–87; use of De Morgan's Law, 98–99, 109; use of prime implicant chart, 97–98, 110; use of truth tables, xiv, 87–89, 105–111, 113–118, 140–143, 162
Boolean algorithms, 85, 97, 110, 116–117, 123–124, 130, 142, 154
Bornschier, Volker, 21, 59
Bradshaw, York, 22
Buraway, Michael, 46–47
Butler, David, 145

Campbell, Donald, 27, 38
Cardoso, Fernando Henrique, 20, 21
Case-oriented research, ix, xiii, 12–13, 16–17, 31, 34–52, 111, 113, 122, 126,

166–168; biases in, ix, 84, 111–112, 127; limitations of, xiii, 49–51, 68
Case-study, 4, 22, 37, 70, 73–74, 76, 79, 80, 82
Categorical data. See Nominal-scale variables
Causal analysis, x, 13, 35
Causal combinations. See Causation, multiple and conjunctural
Causal equivalence, 47, 48, 49, 62–63, 101, 120
Causation: additive models, 25, 32–33, 62–64, 65, 83, 90–91, 106; multiple and conjunctural, x, xii–xiii, 3, 13–15, 23–25, 37–38, 40–41, 42–44, 45–49, 63–64, 65, 78–79, 83, 89–101, 121–122, 126, 166–167; necessary and sufficient conditions, 27, 28, 99–101, 106, 110; structural, 55, 72, 77–78
Chase-Dunn, Christopher, 72, 73
Chemical causation, 24
Chirot, Daniel, 36, 53, 67
Class-voting, 4–5, 9, 14, 125–126
Cluster analysis, 150, 152
Cohen, Lawrence, 150, 169
Collective action, 29, 72–73
Combinatorial logic. See Boolean algebra
Combined causes. See Causation, multiple and conjunctural
Combining methods, xi–xii, xiii–xiv, 17, 33, 69–84
Comparability, problem of, vii–viii, 9, 168–169
Comparative method, 1, 12–16, 31, 78–79, 82–83; and qualitative comparison, 33, 83, 84, 93–101
Comparative social science: distinctiveness of, xi, 2–4, 5–6, 13, 104; divisions within, viii–ix, 171
Comparison, 1, 30–31, 50–51, 78–79, 82–83, 94, 101; Boolean methods, xiv–xv; in experimental designs, 28–29; incomplete, 111
Competition perspective, 135–136, 138–139, 144, 145–146
Complexity, xii–xiii, 18, 19–20, 26, 54, 78, 82, 83, 84, 93, 98, 101, 113, 116–117,

181

Designer:	Mark Ong
Compositor:	G & S Typesetters, Inc.
Text:	10/13 Aldus
Display:	Palatino
Printer:	Braun-Brumfield, Inc.
Binder:	Braun-Brumfield, Inc.